T0354738

**BOOKS BY JAY R. LEACH (Pen name Jay Leach)**

How Should We Then Live
Behold the Man
The Blood Runs Through It
Drawn Away
Give Me Jesus
A Lamp unto My Feet
Grace that Saves
The Narrow Way
Radical Restoration in the Church
Manifestation of the True Children of God
According to Pattern
Battle Cry
Is there not a Cause?
We would See Jesus
According to Pattern 2nd Edition
The Apostolic Rising
For His Glory
Where have all the Shepherds Gone?
Out of Babylon
Living Grace 24/7
When God's Command becomes A Question

# When
# GOD'S
# COMMAND
# *becomes*
# A QUESTION

## HELPING OTHERS TO FOLLOW JESUS

*by Jay Leach*

www.trafford.com
**North America & international**
toll-free: 844-688-6899 (USA & Canada)
fax: 812 355 4082

# CONTENTS

# DEDICATION

*To*
*the precious Christ followers of the Bread of Life Ministries INT'L:*
*The Bread of Life Bible Institute, and our "Flagship," the Bread*
*of Life Church and, also the Bread of Life Church Fellowship.*
*May the truth of God's Word guard your*
*hearts and minds in Christ Jesus,*
*So that you walk in the light as He Himself is in the light.*

*Do not be conformed to this world,*
*but be transformed by the renewing of your mind,*
*so that you may prove what the will of God is,*
*that which is good and acceptable and perfect.*

**Romans 12:2 NASB**

# INTRODUCTION

*"Look carefully then how you walk, not as unwise but as wise, making the best use of the time, because the days are evil. Therefore do not be foolish, but understand what the will of the Lord is."*
Ephesians 5:15-17 ESV

Today people are eager to fight. Especially after they run down the daily news of crime and mayhem on social media. Many are living on the edge, waiting for anyone to make a mistake or misspeak so they can pounce on them. It is in this environment that our Lord tells us to be "eager to maintain unity" (see Ephesians 4:3). It is my prayer that I will write this book with a spirit of unity. While some of the things I write may sound critical, I am really trying to speak in a spirit of love and grace. One of the worst things that could happen is for angry people to take these words and proudly confront their church pastor, or other leadership.

God designed the Church to be much more than what the majority of us experience in the world today. There are many who believe this and desire change. The good news is that God wants this change even more than we do. And He doesn't just want these changes; He *commands* them! One thing we need to get through our "knower" is – we can move forward by faith knowing God wouldn't *command* us to do something unless He anoints and empowers us to get the task done. There is enough division and self-autonomy in the Church already. Certainly, there is a way to show kindness and grace toward one another without abandoning our convictions. Tell the Lord about the difference in your church; and the church you read about.

For those who are in church leadership or those who are not, just keep in mind this is a very difficult time to lead. I have been in leadership positions for more than fifty years. During that period, I conclude there was never a time "such as this for leaders."

Social media gives everyone a voice, so everyone chooses to raise theirs. Voices are plentiful – faithful followers of Christ are not. Strong and varied opinions are applauded – humility is not. I am not saying that changes are not needed, and they should be made, but not without *unity*. Just for a moment, picture in your mind how difficult it would be to coach a team wherein each player refuses to follow because he or she has a better plan than the coach's. This has been the scenario since God created humankind with a "free will to choose." Beginning with the first man and woman created by God, Adam, and Eve, two paths have been laid before humanity – God's plan (a life of dedication and obedience to His will and His way) or (a life of disobedience to the will of God and determining his or her own will and way), apart from God by choice.

God's plan of reconciliation was set in eternity past between God the Father and God the Son whereby rebellious humanity could be redeemed back to God, again by choice. God's plan is presented to humanity in the Bible (His Holy Word). Many people are choosing the natural or humanistic way of life "bloodless sacrifice," which states that there is more than one way to heaven. Rather than accept God's plan through the "blood sacrifice" of His Son. We should be full of faith and anticipation, remembering what He did at the Red Sea and the empty tomb. Satan, the devil, who will be a key player in chapter 1 and throughout this book to demonstrate to you his garden strategy which is his weapon of choice today – that is to change God's commands throughout Scripture to mere questions (did God say?). What deception! To grasp the end of God's story with humanity we must go back to the beginning. If the devil could get rid of the first eleven chapters of the Bible – the rest of the Bible would make little sense. A study guide is located at the end of each chapter to reinforce knowledge of the truth.

Jay Leach
Fayetteville, N.C.

# SECTION ONE
# IT ALL BELONGS TO GOD

# CHAPTER ONE

## One God Intended

*And the Lord God **commanded** the man, "You are free to eat from any tree of the garden, but you must not eat from the tree of the knowledge of good and evil, for on the day you eat from it, you will certainly die." (Genesis 2:16-17 CSB) Emphasis added.*

Much debate has been leveled between various groups concerning the first eleven chapters of the Book of Genesis in the Holy Bible. One says, do not take the chapters literally, another claims they are derived from Greek mythology, etc. However, we do take them literally. If the devil could get rid of these eleven chapters, the rest of the Bible would not make much sense.

Another myth denying these chapters involves a theory of evolution that says: humans evolved [good] in some bog and out of a pagan past; and therefore, ever since their emergence the human race has continually improved itself and thus given rise to the "bloodless sacrifice" of cultural Christianity to which many individual Christians and local churches have succumbed.

## THE TRUTH

The truth of the matter of human origin is found in Genesis 1:26, *"Then God said, let us make man in our image, according to Our likeness; let them have dominion over the fish of the sea, and over the birds of the air, and over the cattle, over all the earth, and over every creeping thing that creeps on the earth."*

The Bible begins, *"In the beginning God created the heaven and the earth."* Creation marks the absolute beginning of the temporal and material world. On the sixth day of creation in contrast to animals in verses 20 and 24 where God said, *"Let the waters bring forth and let the earth bring forth,"* He now says, *"Let us make man in Our image, and according to Our likeness."* Notice all others reproduce after "their kind," but humans are the only ones made in the image of God and reproduces in that image; but though marred by sin, it is still there (see Genesis 3:5).

In creation God placed a great chasm between man and beast, for only man has the capacity for:

- Eternal life
- Fellowship
- Moral discernment
- Self-conscience
- Speech
- Worship

God created man innocent, but not righteous; therefore, he had a choice of obedience as seen in (Genesis 2:16-17).

> And the Lord God commanded the man saying, *"Of every tree of the Garden you may freely eat but of the tree of the knowledge of good and evil, you shall not eat, for in the day that you eat of it you shall surely die."*

## THE FALL OF MAN

Adam and Eve chose, but it was the wrong choice! As a result of their choice, all humanity has suffered from the "fall."

- Human nature is sinful.
- The world is a twisted mess.
- Society has deteriorated at the core.
- Cultures are mingled.
- Religion is reaching up for God who has already come down to us.

We find the reason for this disastrous condition in Genesis 3 – sin! Satan, the father of lies was lurking in the Garden. Where did he come from? He was created one of the highest angels named Lucifer meaning "morning star" or "light bearer." He led an angelic rebellion. Satan chose, but he made the wrong choice.

## THE FALL OF SATAN

He was the original sinner. In Isaiah 14:12, the prophet recorded Satan's boastful prelude to his agenda and fall:

- I will ascend into heaven.
- I will exalt my throne above the stars of God.
- I will also sit upon the mount of the congregation.
- I will ascend above the heights of the clouds.
- I will be like the Highest.

## DECEPTION 101

In Genesis 3:1-4, we read, *Now the serpent was more subtle than the beast of the field which the Lord had made. And he said unto the woman,* **yea, hath God said, ye shall not eat of every tree in the garden?** *And the woman said unto the serpent, we may eat of the fruit of the trees of the garden. But of the fruit of the tree, which is in the midst of the garden, God hath said, Ye shall not eat of it, neither shall you touch it, lest ye die. And the serpent said unto the woman, "Ye shall not surely die."* (KJV). She took away the word "freely" and changed thou shalt surely die from the truth of God's Word and she added to His Word: shall not touch it lest we die.

## SIN ENTERED

The serpent was a creature made by God but used by Satan (see John 8:44; I John 3:8; Revelation 12:9; 20:2). Eve proved to be under the influence of Satan. We can learn much from Eve's encounter with the serpent in that Satan uses the same tricks today in churches. Notice how he deceitfully got Eve to add and subtract from what God had **commanded!** His specialty is to get people to *change truths into* *lies and commands into questions.* The result is doubt and unbelief. Notice his approach, ***"Has God said?"***

When Adam and Eve became disobedient to God's command – sin entered. They sewed fig leaves together to cover their nakedness and shamefully hid from God. Adam and Eve's spiral downward was brought on by disobedience and doubt of God's sincerity. Once doubt sets in then doubt of truth comes. Adam forgot that he owed his very existence to God – his Maker and Sustainer. This made Adam and Eve totally dependent creatures. Humans are not self-existent and therefore cannot be independent. It is in God that "we live and move and have our being" (prayerfully study Acts 17:23-31 NKJV).

## HUMANS ARE MORAL BEINGS

God created humans with a free-will. So that means they are moral beings and therefore responsible. I believe God created the angelic hosts with free-will as well. Freewill means power of choice. God desired that humans would respond to Him willingly and freely.

He placed within each human being a conscience which gives us a moral sense, distinguishing right from wrong in relation to known law. However, conscience is fallible, for since the "fall" of humanity – knowledge has been perverted through sin, therefore, it does not form a perfect basis for judgment.

---

The only true conscience is the truth of God's Word [the Bible] as revealed by the Holy Spirit. Paul explains, the Spirit brings the conscience into alignment with the infallible Word of God (see Romans 9:1).

---

## GOD IS LOVE

God is love and love must have an object which can reciprocate that love (see 1 John 4:16-19). God's answer was the creation of man. Human beings were created by love, for love, and to reciprocate love.

Unless this is us — our heart will remain empty and cold. Therefore, on the Cain side of the "blood line" came "rationalization."[1] One such erroneous conclusion is that in the fall man became deprived except for their mind or intellect. And therefore, intellect enables the person to discern right and wrong through *the five senses.*

For example, with Creation put on the shelf today for evolution theory, science, and secular education, it is apparent that this whole strategy of Satan through human secularism is the "deconstruction" of true Christianity and the Biblical Worldview in the world. The evil thought is, once all of the old is gone — then man can build a new world. Those churches and individual believers who adhere to the truth of God's Word and are daily prayerfully searching the Scriptures will find themselves vulnerable to cultural persecution and temptations of the devil. There is a toxic stench of death in many churches today as many have abandoned the Holy Spirit and the truth of God's Word and have adopted a cultural religion of rationalization, "because everybody is doing it." In the meantime human secularism in its many forms is decimating the *spiritual* foundation pillars of the church (see Jude 3). Human secularists long ago realized that controlling what young people are taught will ultimately determine the philosophical standards of the future in society — this is taking place daily across this country — and in plain sight! Statistically, the rate of moral decay has accelerated more in the present generation than all previous generations combined since the founding of this nation.

Consider, the fact that the United States has become the world's greatest superpower and the depository of Christianity. America has been blessed with more Bible colleges, seminaries, churches, Christian bookstores, Christian television and radio stations than all the rest of the world combined.

---

However, God has never allowed any nation to hold to sin, to the degree that we see in America today and *remain* excluded from judgment.

---

[1] Rationalization is the process of replacing rationally consistent rules for conventional or rather illogical rules with society. Accessed 8/16/23 https.// www.bing.com/search? =what%20theory? & showconv.

This is especially true when people have access to the truth of God's Word available to them as we do. The Bible *warns* that we [all the people] will be held accountable for the resources, and opportunities; that God has given us:

> *"And that servant who knew his master's will and didn't prepare himself or do it will be severely beaten. But the one who did not know and did what deserved punishment will receive a light beating. From everyone who has been given much, much will be required; and from the one who has been entrusted with much, even more will be expected."* (Luke 12:47-48 CSB)

This means we cannot live as though we will not have to pay a price for our sins and resulting consequences – in spite of the atrocious past our fore-parents experienced to subsequent generations,[2] essentially today's rising toxic atmosphere of denial, lies, and rationalization on the part of governmental leadership. Some people are just wishing it will just go away, but it can't. When we ignore our mistakes of the past, it's just a matter of time before we repeat them. Like Rome which history reports, was never totally destroyed by an outside enemy but from within, then it moved into the shadows, to periodically appear in some form.

Sadly, in our coming together today, fewer of our brothers and sisters look to Almighty God through Jesus Christ, our Savior, as so many of our fore parents did. Many people have determined for our own generation's future, and because we have not arrived (naturally) many are abandoning a biblical worldview, the True and Living God, and the gospel of Christ for a cultural Christianity, idolatry, other ideologies and religions of the world?

Doctrine is the gauge of the Christian life. It is what orients disciples in a disorienting world. As the church fails to give the people theology, we are abandoning them to trust their intuition in the darkness of the world. We are telling them that they don't need to receive instructions and direction from anything or anybody other

---

2    Jay Leach, *We Would See Jesus* (Trafford Publishing 2020) 117

6

than what *they* feel is right in their own eye – and much of what they have to offer is self-destructing.

---

## MISGUIDED BELIEFS LEAD TO A MISGUDED LIFE!

---

# THE STATE OF THEOLOGY SURVEY IN THE U.S. (2014-2020)

In 2020, Lifeway Research and Ligonier Ministries released a research project on "The State of Theology."[3] This research is meant to help local churches understand the current theological temperature of the church.

The results were staggering:

The church is confused about who God is, what it means to be an image-bearer, who Christ is, what sin is, what salvation is, and much more. People were largely confused about the person of Christ.

When asked to agree or disagree with the statement "Jesus is the first and greatest being created by God," a fourth century heresy known as Arianism, 78% (percent) agreed. The church is also largely confused about the *exclusivity* of Christ. When asked to agree or disagree that "God accepts the worship of all religions, including Christianity, Judaism, and Islam," 51% (percent) agreed.

One more example: When asked to agree or disagree, "Everyone sins a little, but most people are good by nature," a heresy known as Pelagianism, 52% (percent) agreed.

---

[3]   "The State of Theology," The State of Theology, accessed April 7, 2020, https// thestateoftheology.com.

# THE STATE OF THEOLOGY SURVEY IN THE U.S. (2014-2022)

According to the latest State of Theology survey (2022)[4] the clearest and most consistent trend since 2014 has been erosion in Americans' confidence that the Bible is literally true. Ever since Satan appeared in the garden of Eden, he has sought to undermine faith in God's Word. Theological liberalism follows that same strategy and continually casts doubt on the Bible: Does God mean what He says? The Bible answers emphatically yes, bearing clear testimony to its truthfulness and accuracy (Psalms 12:6; 119:160; 2 Timothy 3:16). You would rightly be upset if a fellow church member told you:

- That God changes His plans in response to events on earth.
- That humans are essentially good.
- That Jesus was a good teacher but not God.

# THREE NEW QUESTIONS

Three new questions were featured in the latest survey. Each revealed alarming answers:

1.  *God learns and adapts to different circumstances.* The living God as revealed in Scripture, knows all things and is unchanging (see Ps. 147:5; Mal. 3:6; Rom. 11:33-34; James 1:17). Yet 51 percent of American adults agreed with the statement.
2.  *Everyone is born innocent in the eyes of God.* All mankind fell in Adam, and so all his descendants are born sinners (see Romans 5:12; Ps. 51:5). Yet 71 percent of adults agree with the statement.
3.  *Every Christian has an obligation to join a local church.* It is assumed in the New Testament that followers of Jesus Christ will gather together in local congregations. Christians join together in local churches to worship God, to receive the

---

4   https//tablemagazine.com/article/2023/01/the-stateof-theglogy2022#5text=Ligo nie/%20coxces%20the%bienial% Accessed on 9/8/23.

means of grace, and for fellowship with one another. Yet people today in the West too often regard this as a lifestyle choice, with only 36 percent of American adults agreeing. The fact that this percentage was not higher may have been influenced by a variety of factors, including restrictions on church attendance during the coronavirus pandemic and the widespread online viewing of church service.

The percentage of U.S. adults agreeing with the statement "The Bible, like all sacred writings, contains helpful accounts of ancient myths but is not literally true" rose from 41 percent in 2014 to 53 percent in 2022.[5]

It is no surprise that a rising tide of secularization happens as trust in the Bible declines. There are some clear indications of this in the survey. For example, an increasing number of U. S. adults agree with the statement "God is unconcerned with my day-to-day decisions" (32 percent in 2022).

We are also witnessing a growing *rejection* of God's created order. The idea that gender identity is something that people choose is now supported by 42 percent of the American population. A higher percentage than previously (46 percent) agree that "The Bible's condemnation of homosexual behavior doesn't apply today." Like the sons of Issachar, as Christ followers we must sense the urgency of the times.[6]

For the sake of the family and the Christian Church, our children, our grands and great grandchildren we must do all we can to insure they chose to serve the Lord. Satan, the prince of this world, has effectively distorted and progressively undermined our Christian values in this generation.

God tells us in His Word, *"My people perish for a lack of [Biblical] knowledge."* [Bracket is mine]. We do well to stop, study, pray and learn from what happened in the days of Noah. Then take positive action. The Scriptures reveal that a time will come when God will no longer be sympathetic to the cries of America or any other country that turns

---

[5]  Ibid.
[6]  1 Chronicles 12:32

their back on Him. Speaking through the prophet Jeremiah, Then the Lord said to me,

> *"Even if Moses and Samuel stood before Me, my mind would not be favorable toward this people. Cast them out of My sight and let them go forth"* (Jermiah 15:1 NKJV).

The very same concept was expressed to Ezkiel, *"The word of the LORD came again to me saying: "Son of man, when a land sins against Me by persistent unfaithfulness, I will stretch out My hand against it; I will cut off its supply of bread, send famine on it, and cutoff man and beast from it. Even if these three men, Noah, Daniel, and Job, were in it, they would deliver only themselves by their righteousness,"* says the Lord GOD" (Ezekiel 14:12-14 NKJV).

## WHAT SATAN CANNOT DESTROY – HE CONTAMINATES

I believe Satan really experienced his limitations when he instigated the rebellion among the angels, which resulted in him and those angels who chose to follow him – being kicked out of heaven. The intensity of his evil deeds and deceptions throughout the ages could lead some to believe, including himself, that he might still have a chance to win. However, the cross and the resurrection of Jesus Christ fulfilling (the promises of Genesis 3:15) should have convinced him of the futility of his dream of taking the seat of the Most High God. Knowing that he has but a short time, Satan has set a course to deceive, distort, and destroy the present and future generations and what he cannot destroy he contaminates. Because the apostle Paul does not want Satan to deceive the church he directs and exhorts certain maneuvers and actions for them [the entire church] to execute!

# A CALL TO THE ENTIRE BODY OF CHRIST

Paul specifically defines the nature of the essential ministry of the Word that is the calling of every member of the body of Christ. Notice his Spirit-guided counsel to all members in the church in Colossians 3:15-17:

> *"And let the peace of God rule in your hearts, to which also you were called in one body; and be thankful. Let the Word of Christ dwell in you richly in all wisdom, teaching and admonishing one another in psalms and hymns and spiritual songs, singing with grace in your hearts to the Lord. And whatever you do in word and deed, do all in the name of the Lord Jesus, giving thanks to God the Father through Him."* (NKJV)

Paul visualizes a well-discipled church with the Word of God dwelling in their hearts – wide awake and positioned to do God's "will" as He has established in His Word for the whole body to do. Again, Paul is very specific about the body's God-given assignment: *teaching* and *admonishing*. He is proposing that every believer is designated to have a ministry of teaching. This "ministry of all believers" is an "all of God's people all of the time" kingdom mission. It is apparent here that any church is unhealthy and vulnerable, if the pastor is the only teacher.

So, no matter where God has placed the teacher in the body of Christ, it is absolutely essential that he or she be discipled (taught to maturity), and everyone being taught – need also to teach! Being a pastor and Bible teacher myself, I know first-hand the need for the pastor to be surrounded by faithful, matured, well-trained teachers (discipled) and graceful admonishers. The NIV Bible lists about fifty statements that I call "one another ministries," which call us to a special kind of life together – for all in the body.

In fact, the New Testament puts much emphasis on the need for all Christians including pastors and other leaders to know one another closely and intimately enough to be able to bear one another's burdens, confess our faults one to another, encourage, exhort, and admonish one another – to minister to one another with the Word, song, and prayer.

Many of today's local churches have managed to do away with the true New Covenant biblical Christianity and have substituted cultural Christianity's one or two sermons a month to get the job done. Such churches have completely reduced their churches' witness and influence. Thus, they have removed the major safeguard to the health of the churches' spirituality and growth within and greatly weakened their effectiveness in the eyes of the world outside. So many dying churches follow this same pattern today. While many try to turn to the blame game, or to rationalization and secular programs, the real culprit in this cultural expulsion of God, Christ, and the Holy Spirit with His gifts and ministries – is the church itself.

Although we feed from the banquet table of truth with our family and friends once a week, we remain silent and uninvolved in the lives of our co-workers in the marketplace, lost family members, friends and neighbors. We have remained silent and uninvolved in their lives. Does our "daily walk" align with our biblical "talk?"

---

If we ignore the crying relational needs of our neighbors, we cannot expect them to be attracted to the message of the Gospel.

---

The reason most people know so little of God today is because the Christians they know have developed amnesia when it comes to communicating Jesus to them through righteous living. This silence advances the devil's agenda to kill *truth anywhere he finds it.* Thus, in John 8:44, Jesus describes the devil as both a liar and a murderer. Jesus said it and that settles it. He says,

> *"He was a murderer from the beginning, and does not stand in truth, because there is no truth in him. When he speaks a lie, he speaks from his own, for he is a liar and the father of it."* NKJV

---

"Our very life depends on a daily diet of the Word of God!"

---

# VOLUNTARY IGNORANCE

Voluntary spiritual and biblical ignorance have changed the way some Christians speak of Satan, in some instances they speak as if he is above God. Others in their worldly enlightenment do not believe the devil or his demons exist. But Scripture assures us that Christ defeated him through His death and His resurrection according to *promise:* (also called the 1ˢᵗ Gospel or Proto Evangel verse)

> *"And I will put enmity.*
> *Between you and the woman,*
> *And between your seed and her*
> *Seed.*
> *He shall bruise your head.*
> *And you shall bruise His heal."*
> Genesis 3:15 ESV

Yes, the God of time and eternity had already experienced the crisis of Calvery. He already experienced the heart-piercing pain of His Son's separation from Him. This is no doubt the reason He could say to Adam, "I know experientially what it means to be alone. From eternity past I have known the pain and emptiness of My Son's being separated from Me. Adam, I know about being alone – and it is not good." Live in God's love as you contemplate the question: Why did He do it? God allowed this agonizing separation because you and I were alone, and He wanted to remove our aloneness!

Ever since the fall of Adam and Eve, the human family has been alienated and separated from God. But God whose heart is rich in grace and mercy, went through incredible lengths to restore the fellowship interrupted by sin. Reconciliation could take place only if a remedy for sin was made possible. So, Jesus Christ, the Son of God:

- willingly took on a robe of flesh,
- suffered the relational pain of humiliation, and rejection,
- died a criminal's death, and,
- in becoming sin,

He experienced the aching void of separation from His Father, which He did for you and for me. In so doing, He made provision for both our fallenness and our aloneness. God almighty personally suffered the separation caused by our sin. So, coming to the church (the body of Christ) there is One God! If we would be honest with ourselves, we would have to admit that in actuality within our local church we find two separate theologies concerning our God and Christianity. We will label them biblical Christianity and an opposing cultural Christianity.

## BIBLICAL CHRISTIANITY

Biblical Christianity is not a religion, but it is the abundant life Christ promised. This life of faith starts and ends with God. It starts and ends with the idea that nothing is better than God and that He has given Himself to us in Jesus Christ and in the gospel.

As human beings, our instinct is to magnify how great we are, but as Christ followers, we are learning to proclaim, "O magnify the LORD with me, and let us exalt His name together!" (see Psalm 34:3) Christianity is not about self-improvement – it is a discipleship growth of self-denial. You will know yourself the most when you are carrying your own cross. The way of Jesus, an apprenticeship toward *self-forgetfulness,* a growing *understanding* that we are the creation and God is the Creator. One writer expressed it, He is perfect, and we are both beautiful as image-bearers and broken as sinners. That He is the Redeemer, and we are in need of redemption. Give Him praise and glory! I love the old hymn of the church "Yes, God is Real!" Yes, biblical Christianity is not about a path to self-improvement; it is a path of self-denial that leads to a cross.

## CULTURAL CHRISTIANITY

Preparing to discuss our next topic, cultural Christianity, I am reminded of the prophet Habakkuk's words to the people of God: "For the earth *will be filled* with the knowledge of the glory of the LORD as the waters cover the sea." (Habakkuk 2:14 ESV) He writes these words as God's people are *questioning* God's use of Assyria and Babylon to bring judgment upon them. Their kingdom is in shambles, they are practicing idolatry and deep wickedness, and they are full of questions:

What are God's purposes in all of this?
Can this really be it?
Is exile in Babylon going to be our final destiny?
Where is all of this heading?
What is the goal of the world?

This is the prophet's answer: *One day the whole earth, every single part of it – the sky, the mountains, the rivers, the canyons, all creatures, and all peoples – will be filled with the knowledge of the glory of the Lord.* Not only will it fill them, but it will fill them as the waters cover the sea.

This is a picture of where world history seems to be heading. I see the picture of the destruction of Gaza today as a comparative of what this whole world is coming to. At the same time as with the prophet in the middle of the darkest hour, a time of judgment the prophet reminds God's people everywhere, that all world history is heading toward the kingdom and the *endless* presence of God.

Someone may be asking so what does that mean? Where is Leach going with all of this? People across the church are crying, "we are losing our spirituality" in the church. What we are witnessing is the fact that this country and the West are caught up in a cultural moment that centers *all of reality* on the autonomous self. People's interest in spirituality is not waning (going down) but the *kind of spirituality* that people want is increasingly (going up), a spirituality that is focused on the *self.*

Sadly, in this turn to self the church has perhaps both intentionally and unintentionally tailored its discipleship strategies to accommodate, and perpetuate this cultural shift. Within the past month (December 2023) Pope Francis sanctioned same sex blessings for (13:4 billion Catholics worldwide). A few days later the Anglican church's top leader sanctioned same sex blessings (1.36 billion Anglicans worldwide). Certainly this is a global assault on the truth of the Bible (the Word of God). Both of these churches influence billions of people globally to include (69,000 Anglicans in the US).[7] Needless to say, these (decisions of compromise) have created divisions in their churches. Several Anglican bishops from Africa, Asia, Latin America, and the Pacific said after the decision that they no longer recognize Archbishop of Canterbury Justin Welby as their leader. Certainly, other non-affiliated church denominations are going to follow their cultural Christianity lead.

In other words it is God and God alone, that is man's highest good in (biblical Christianity) but now it is contrasted with a contemporary cultural Christianity mantra: "Self, and being true to yourself *alone,* is your highest good."

---

## REPLACING THE TRANCENDANCE OF GOD WITH THE TRANCENDANCE OF SELF.

---

Ever since Genesis 3 human beings have viewed the knowledge of self as the highest good, **falsely** believing that the self, not God, is the bottomless well of beauty. Salvation, according to self-centered cultural Christianity, is not found in knowing God but in knowing self. At every turn today, we are being told that truly finding ourselves is the antidote to our stress, anxiety, and confusion, but biblical Christianity says Christ is the antidote.

In other words, it is not just the secularist promise that salvation is found in self-improvement, self-actualization, and self-growth, but this is slowly becoming the promise of the church also. The appearance of this self-centered cultural Christianity has caused serious division and confusion about who God is, and what the church's role is.

In Matthew 16, Jesus confronts this view of discipleship self-improvement. So, what does it look like when we succumb to the "lie" that discipleship is about being true to yourself?

---

This results when our churches and ministries begin to offer people what they want instead of what they need.

---

[7] The statistics concerning the Catholic church, the Anglican church and the Anglican U.S. populations from Jill Lawless Associated Press/ FAYOBSERVER. COM (December 19, 2023).

This happens when disciples don't have a first-hand knowledge of their sacred text, or basic Christian beliefs, but have an abundance of knowledge of politics, sports, or entertainment. Herein the disciple is more shaped by practices and habits of secularism than basic spiritual disciplines.

## STUDY GUIDE: CHAPTER 1

1. The purpose of the Incarnation was to offer a plan of _____ to all who would receive it.

2. _____ and _____ remain God's New Testament strategy for the body of Christ.

3. We have experienced the _____ _____ in the universe.

4. We are missing something absolutely _____ for a true church (spiritual maturity) because of a _____ of _____ for _____ _____.

5. Explain what is meant by _____ of _____.

6. Explain why Hebrews 10:25 is so important.

7. Jesus' prayer was not for us to just get along _____ His prayer was that we become _____ _____.

# CHAPTER TWO

# God's Love And Mercy

*For God so loved the world in this way: He gave his one and only Son, so that everyone who believes in him will not perish but have eternal life.* (John 3:16 CSB)

Islam and many other religions do not believe that Jesus is the unique Son of God. According to the Koran, "No son did God beget, nor is there any God along with him" (Surah 23:91). But on nine occasions the Bible refers to Jesus as the begotten Son of the Father. Not only did God declare Him to be His Son at His baptism (see Luke 3:23), but He also proved it by raising Jesus from the dead (see Romans 1:4). Throughout the New Testament, and especially in the Book of John, as he draws special attention to, "Sonship" in reference to the intimate spiritual relationship between God and Jesus. The purpose of the Incarnation[8] was to <u>offer a plan of salvation to all who would receive it.</u> (see John 3:3; 3:16) Those who refuse it simply remain in the condemned state they were already in (see John 3:17).

---

"There are only two kinds of people in the end: Those who say to God, 'Thy will be done – and those to whom God says, 'Thy will be done.'"
— C. S. Lewis

---

[8] The biblical definition of incarnation is the belief that God became human in the person of Jesus Christ, who is both fully God and fully man. This is an act of grace by God to reveal Himself to humanity for its salvation. Incarnation is a key doctrine of the Christian faith and the Trinity, as it affirms that Jesus is the eternal Word or Son of God, who was conceived by the Holy Spirit in the womb of the virgin Mary. Accessed 8/20/23 https//www.Biblestudytools.com/dictionary/incarnation-Jesus-Christ.

# HAS OLD-TIME RELIGION BEEN CANCELED?

We hear and have read much about the emptiness or conversion of former church buildings across Europe where young people especially students have never heard of God or Jesus, nor do they have any concept of who or what He is. Periodically, this situation is aired here in the U.S., we hear the response, "How could they let that happen?" It might surprise you to know, the same is true for the most part here in North America, in the present generations among our millennials, Gen Zers, and soon to arrive the alpha generation. Although some of them have grown up in church and regularly attended youth ministries and Sunday school yet have no real knowledge of Jesus Christ or the Bible. Many sermons today are concerned with politics, prosperity and/or entertainment. Some pastors have chosen to not speak of sin, repentance, the blood of Jesus, His resurrection, eternal life or eternal punishment. Yet, they are continuously applauded for such an inspiring, but never challenging message.

In other churches basic Bible knowledge is missing or blended with Eastern or so many other spiritualities that true biblical redemption in Jesus Christ has almost become obscure. This is obvious in the way churches are striving to survive, today after having neglected or simply thrown away a generation of youth and young adults, while at the same time abolishing biblical marriage and the family. Biblical "teaching and admonishing" remain God's New Testament strategy for the body of Christ.

# SUPERNATURAL LOVE

The New Testament makes it clear that the church is supposed to be known for its love. According to Jesus our love for "one another" is the very thing that will attract the world. Can you name a single church in your community that is known for the way its members love one another? Certainly, we can think of churches known for powerful preaching or worship. Praise God for that! But the question remains, can you name a church known for its supernatural love?

In the New Testament we find numerous mentions of the phrase "one another" (love one another, care for one another… admonish one another ... teach one another... pray for one another...etc.), yet we can hardly find a church known for the way they take care of one another. Why is this? In most cases, the love in our churches is a far cry from anything that we could attribute to the Holy Spirit.

Sometimes we claim that we have "Christian love" in our church, yet we probably show more love to coworkers, and neighbors outside. Jesus made it clear that even sinners know how to love one another (see Luke 6:32-34). However, our love experience must far exceed any of these.

Jesus said, *"As I have loved you, you also are to love one another."* (John 13:34) Jesus Christ, our Savior and Lord, who allowed Himself to be tortured and killed for us – tells us to love one another in the same way. Have you ever thought of loving a fellow Christian brother or sister as sacrificially and selflessly as Christ loved you? Have you looked at a brother or sister *selflessly* lately, wanting to bring him or her to life – no matter the cost? Picture the faces of a few of the people in your church and imagine the way Jesus thought of each of those people as He hung there on the cross. No sacrifice was too great, holding nothing back – He did all that was necessary to redeem, heal and transform those specific people. He did the same thing for yourself, now, who does God want you to pursue? Think about it, Jesus pursued those people from heaven to earth to bring them into His family. What barriers could keep you from seeking a familial relationship with them? We have *experienced* the greatest love in all the universe. Shouldn't that have focused the love of Jesus to flow out of us? Shouldn't that be enough to influence the world around us?

> *"Beloved, let us love one another, for love is from God,*
> *and whoever loves has been born of God and knows God.*
> *Anyone who does not love does not know God,*
> *because God is love. In this the love of God was made*
> *manifest among us, that God sent his only Son into*
> *the world, so that we might live through him. In this*
> *is love, not that we have loved God but that he loved*
> *us and sent his son to be the propitiation for our sins.*
> *Behold, if God so loved us, we also ought to love one*
> *another. No one has ever seen God; if we love one another,*
> *God abides in us, and his love is perfected in us."*

1 John 4:7-12 ESV

**Note the promise here!** *If we love one another,* God will *abide* in us, and His love will be *perfected* (matured) in us. We live like this statement is too good to be true, but it is true! This thinking is so painful, because there is also an important *warning* in this passage – that those who don't love don't know God. Have we missed this warning?

There is certainly a message here for our church leadership today. Where have we missed it? The importance of loving one another is emphasized all throughout Scripture:

*Let love be genuine.*
*Abhor what is evil; hold fast to what is good.*
*Love one another with brotherly affection.*
*Outdo one another in showing honor.*
Romans 12:9-10 ESV

*If I speak in the tongues of angels, but have not love,*
*I am a noisy gong or a clanging cymbal.*
1 Corinthians 13:1 ESV

*Above all, keep loving one another earnestly,*
*since love covers a multitude of sins.*
1 Peter 4:8 ESV

We are missing something absolutely essential for a true church, (spiritual maturity) because of our lack of love for "one another."

---

If we love one another, God will *abide in us,* and His love will be perfected in us.

---

# THE HEART OF THE PROBLEM

We are the body of Christ, ordained by God to proclaim the Good News. So why do we have so little impact on a hurting world, not to mention our own members and leaders. Much research reflects that the culture no longer sees us as a *relevant*[9] *solution* to its needs because we have lost touch with the very heart of who we are. As the people of God, we may hold:

- The right views on sin, embrace the right concepts of truth, and proclaim the right steps to salvation.
- Listen, if we are out of touch with why we do what we do, our churches and ministries will be *irrelevant*[10] to this dying world. So, to whatever extent we are irrelevant to the world around us – is not God's fault!
- I believe this is the reason why hurtful people are not running to our churches and ministries today – where the solutions to their deepest needs can be met.
- Additionally, it is the reason so many of our church members are hurting and unfulfilled.
- The Gospel is the relevant solution to humankind's deepest needs.

Jesus was asked which commandment was the greatest. He answered, *"You shall love the Lord your God with all your heart, and with all your soul, and with all your mind.' This is the greatest and foremost commandment. The second is like it, 'You shall love your neighbor as yourself.' On these two commandments depend on the whole Law and the Prophets."* (Matthew 22:37-40 NASB). The Great Commandment *to love God and to love people* defines the true identity of those who are

---

[9] According to Webster, something is relevant when it has "significant and demonstrable bearing on the matter at hand." A relevant solution is clearly applicable and pertinent, significantly impacting the needs of the current situation.

[10] A solution that does not meet the *obvious need* is deemed irrelevant.

called His Church. Great Commandment love is (God's will for *all* of those who are His), the heart of who we are and what we do.[11]

God and His eternal Word are relevant to the needs of every relationship, every culture, and every period of history – including the present!

When we live out (God's will and commands for us), this principle of loving God and others we minister to *aloneness* in the human heart. The story is told of a pastor who stood up and barely began his sermon when a side door open and in stepped a bedraggled "street person," he looked around and saw no available seat, so he moved forward and sat down on the floor in front of the altar. The preacher ignored him and tried to continue his sermon. Parishioners held a collective breath staring at the man. Soon, one of the older deacons got up and walked over to where the man was seated smiling, he plopped down beside him, welcoming him to the service – there they remained until the service was over.

The people settled down – this removal of aloneness that is vital to our ministry to those in the church and to those who are unchurched. It has been proven with church after church, we cannot effectively do what we are called to do unless *we* embrace and live out our identity as people who love God and others. In fact, when we stick to the Great Commandment principle of loving God and one another, we can "do" church effectively because we are "being" His Church.

In response to the statement "Worshipping alone or with one's family is a valid replacement for regularly attending church" increased from 52 percent agreement in 2014 to 66 percent in 2022. In the context of pandemic restrictions, it is easy to see why acceptance of online options would increase. Biblical Christians, however, cannot endorse the general drift away from *in-person church attendance* for worship. The book of Hebrews explicitly warns us not to give up meeting together (see Hebrews 10:25). Let's not forget that around the world today, some of our brothers and sisters in Christ are risking their lives by gathering together for worship. Americans are increasingly rejecting the divine origin and complete accuracy of the Bible. It is also important to note, with no plumb line of absolute truth to conform to,

---

[11] Adapted from the book, *The Never Alone Church,* David Ferguson (Tyndale House Publishers, Inc. 1998) 8.

U.S. adults are also increasingly holding unbiblical worldviews, related to human sexuality.

## THE GREAT COMMISSION

Equally important with the Great Commandment is the Great Commission: *"Go therefore and make disciples of all the nations, baptizing them in the name of the Father and the Son and the Holy Spirit, teaching them to observe all that I commanded you."* (Matthew 28:19-20 NASB) While the Great Commandment to love God and others defines our heart (who we are) as the church. The Great Commission declares God's truth on sin, Scripture, and salvation, which relates more to the mission of the church. The Great Commission defines what we do. The two works in tandem with each other.

When we live out this combined principle, we accomplish the Great Commission within the context of the Great Commandment. This principle will bring the evidence of God's love into every relationship we enjoy. Our churches become testimonies of His love, a place where those entering will no longer feel alone.

## SUPERNATURAL CHURCH UNITY

When Jesus came near to the end of His earthly life, He prayed for His disciples. He prayed that the *unity* of His followers would be equal to the *oneness* of the Father and Son! Often, we call the passage in Matthew 6 the Lord's prayer. However, a closer look reveals that He was teaching His disciples to pray. Later, we are challenged in John 17, where without a doubt what He prayed was truly the Lord's prayer. His desire is that you and I be one just as the Father and Son are One.

> *"I do not ask for these only, but for those who will*
> *believe in me through their word, that they may all be*
> *one, just as you Father, are in me, and I in you, that*
> ***that you have sent me.*** *The glory that you have*
> *given me I have given to them, that they may be one*
> *even as we are one, I in them and you in me, that they may*

> *become perfectly one, so that the world may know that*
> *you sent me and loved them even as you loved me."*
> John 17:20-23 ESV Emphasis is mine.

Have you and your church ever considered pursuing this type of unity (supernatural unity)? Jesus did not pray that we would just get along. His prayer was that we become **"perfectly one."** He prayed this because our oneness was designed to be the way to prove that Jesus was the Messiah. I repeat here for emphasis: Jesus said the purpose for <u>our unity</u> was *"so that the world may know that you sent me and loved them."*

For many today this prayer doesn't make sense. How can our unity result in the world's belief? How can seeing us love one another make someone believe that Jesus truly came from heaven? It's supernatural! Remember the law of first mention in studying the Word of God:

- God spoke and the world came into existence.
- The children of Israel obediently marched around the city wall seven times and the wall fell down (see Joshua 6).
- You shall receive power after the Holy Spirit comes upon you (see Acts 1:8).
- Church unity doesn't seem as if it would result in getting people saved, but it actually did happen (see Acts 2:44-47).

The Book of Acts describes the (how) and extent of their unity:

> *"Now the full number of those who believed were of*
> *one heart and soul, and no one said that any of the*
> *things that belonged to him were his own, but they had*
> *everything in common. And **with great power** the*
> *apostles were giving their testimony to the resurrection*
> *of the Lord Jesus, and **great grace** was upon them all.*
> *There was not a needy person among them, for as many as*
> *were owners of lands or houses sold them and brought*
> *the proceeds of what was sold and laid it at the apostles'*
> *feet, and it was distributed to each as any had need."*
> Acts 4:32-35 ESV Emphasis added.

That passage of Scripture always fires me up. The Church looks so beautiful. It is this kind of love that makes our message believable. Scripture is truly clear: there is a real connection between our unity and the believability of our message. If we are serious about winning the lost we must be serious about pursuing unity.

---

Church, if we are serious about winning the lost – we must be serious about pursuing unity.

---

*"Only let your manner of life be worthy of the gospel of Christ, so that whether I come and see you or am absent, I may hear of you that you are standing firm in one spirit, with one mind striving side by side for the faith of the gospel, and not frightened in anything by your opponents. This is a clear sign to them of their destruction, but of your salvation, and that from God."*
Philippians 1:27-28 ESV

We are living in a day when very few people believe in the wrath of God. Even the vilest people we know have no fear of a literal judgment day coming. If you have tried to convince such a person of their future destruction then, you know what I'm talking about. It's not an easy task. Yet Scripture tells us that our *fearless unity* will convince them!

Paul's emphasis on unity may suggest some division within the Philippian congregation. As the Philippians maintain courage in the face of their opponents, these opponents will find that such remarkable strength could only come from God, and thus anyone who continues to oppose God's people will be marked for destruction. But God's sustaining grace amid trouble will assure the believers of their own salvation. Paul follows the teaching of Jesus here reminding them that persecution is a sign that they belong to Christ. They are to live as lights in the world.

# STUDY GUIDE: CHAPTER 2

1. The purpose for the Incarnation was to offer a _____ of _____ to all who would receive it.
2. _____ and _____ remains God's New Testament strategy for the body of Christ.
3. We have experienced the _____ _____ in the universe.
4. We are missing something absolutely _____ for a true church (spiritually matured) because of a _____ of _____ for _____ _____.
5. Explain what is meant by removal of aloneness is.
6. Why is Hebrew 10:25 so important.
7. Jesus' prayer was not for us to just get along _____ His prayer was that we become _____ _____.

# CHAPTER THREE

## Discipleship Is Not Evangelism

*"Remember your leaders, those who spoke to
you the word of God. Consider the outcome of
their way of life and imitate their faith."*
Hebrews 13:7 ESV

Do you really think that God is pleased when His children chose to be silent at such a time as this? By choosing to do so, simply demonstrates the cowardice that masquerades through much of the church as "godly meekness." "Don't rock the boat!" "Leave it alone!" "This too shall pass!" These and many such haunting similarities have rapidly become the norm across the wide spectrum of the American Church today.

Such silence is not justified at any place or point in the Scriptures. However, our people are so vulnerable toward the traditions of men, and lacking in the knowledge of the truth, that the "lie" in about any situation is acceptable. Sadly, in many pulpits even knowing the truth, many leaders still shrink from combatting the evils of our day.

---

**"Silence is the face of evil and is itself evil. Not to speak is to speak. Not to act is to act. God will not hold us guiltless."[12]**
**Attributed to Dietrich Bonhoeffer**

---

[12] Eric Metaxas, *Letter to the American Church:* (Published by Salem Books, Washington, D.C. 2022)

## BE SILENT NO MORE

We must admonish and exhort our fellow Christians to repent of their chosen silence in the face of growing evil. Mothers and fathers are hurting and sorrowing over their children as they see their rights as parents slipping away from them across this country as national, state, and local governments, politics, along with social media accept it as a progressive move. Christians must refute the pernicious "lie" that fighting evil politicizes Christianity. Metaxas lists four principal ways in which our misunderstanding has helped us to reach this unpleasant place of error.[13] Throughout the centuries heroes of the faith have insisted, the Church has an irreplaceable role not only in the local culture, but in the culture of this nation.

Some time ago, I came across an illustration of an old man *standing* with his old, sway-backed horse beside him. A group of mischievous young boys came along laughing at the sight. They began to chide the old man concerning the old ugly horse, "Can he run?" "Can he do tricks?" Irritatingly he bellowed, "HE CAN STAND!"

In the last chapter, we saw demonstrated, the power of *fearless unity.* Paul reminds the Philippian Church that persecution is a sign that they belong to God. I can't emphasize enough – that our fearless unity will convince them. We must put on our spiritual armor and join the fray against evil and the present darkness. We are to *live* as lights in a world gone wild. We must stand!

---

[13] Adapted from Metaxas' book, *Letter to the American Church,* pages 53-54. 1) is the error of misunderstanding the meaning of the word" faith," which we have cheapened, and which is directly related to Bonhoeffer's idea of "cheap grace." 2) the second error has to do with what he call the "idol of evangelism." This is the unbiblical idea that the only real role the church has is evangelism. So we must never say anything that might in any way detract from our pursuing this single goal. 3) This error may be summed up by the false commandment "Be Ye Not Political," leading to the idea that politics are off limits and beyond the boundaries of our faith. 4) the fourth and final error on the list is the pietistic and perfectly negative idea that our Christian faith is lived out principally by avoiding sin, so that we must place our own virtue and salvation above all other matters.

# DISCIPLES OF CHRIST

Many people confuse discipleship and evangelism, thinking they are the same. A closer look reveals that evangelism's concerns is the "new birth" and justification; whereas discipleship is about witness, sanctification and "spiritual maturity." The word "disciple" occurs 296 times in the New Testament, while "Christian" is found 3 times. Disciple was first introduced to and refer precisely to the disciples of Jesus. This occurred in a situation when it was no longer possible to regard them as sect of the Jews. *"And in Antioch the disciples were first called Christians."* (Acts 11:26 ESV).

The New Testament is a book about disciples, made by disciples for Jesus Christ. But the point is not merely *verbal*. What is more important is that *the kind of life* we see in the earliest church is that of a special type of person. All of the assurances, and benefits offered to humankind in the Gospel evidently presupposes *such a life* and does not make realistic sense apart from it.

The disciple of Jesus Christ is not the deluxe or heavy-duty model of the Christian – especially padded, textured, streamlined, and empowered for the fast lane on the straight and narrow way. He or she stands on the pages of the New Testament as the first level of basic transportation in the kingdom of God.

## Do we trust God?

---

Discipleship is not a path to *autonomous* self-improvement that leads to a throne – it is a path of *self-denial* that leads to a cross.

---

Our people are being sold on all kinds of visions of the good (abundant) life. They are being constantly *formed* through books, social media, and podcasts into their idea of the abundant life. The Christian faith tells us, the abundant life starts and ends with God. It starts and ends with the idea that nothing is better than God and that He has given Himself to us in Christ and in the gospel. Our churches must not settle for a Christianized version of cultural discipleship, self-actualization, or self-improvement when we can have God instead.

Isn't that the real issue in our churches today? We say that Jesus defeated death on the Cross. We confess that we died with Him on the Cross and now in Him we have life. But God knows whether we actually believe it or are just claiming to. He sees it in our life and actions. God asks us:

- Will you trust Me with your finances?
- Will you trust Me with your life?
- Will you trust Me with the life of your wife and children?

God is not necessarily pleased by what we say we "believe." Do we think our friends and neighbors are fooled by what we say we believe? People see precisely what we believe – by how we behave. Do you believe what God says?

One of the greatest challenges facing the church today is discipleship that centers on the autonomous self. People's interest in spirituality is not weakening, but the kind of spirituality people are increasingly interested in is a spirituality that is focused on the "self." The claim that "God and God alone, is your highest good." We have replaced the transcendence of God with the transcendence of *self.*

Though this problem is uniquely clear in our cultural moment it is nor a new problem. As we saw earlier in Genesis 3 humans have viewed the love and knowledge of self as our highest good. Falsely believing that salvation is not found in knowing God but in knowing self. We are being told everywhere that truly finding ourselves is the antidote to our stress, anxiety, and confusion, but biblical discipleship says knowledge of God is the only *true* antidote. True self-knowledge comes not through being true to yourself but through denying yourself.

---

When we make discipleship about *self-actualization,* not *self-denial,* we fail to embody the way of the cross that Jesus commands His followers to imitate.

---

Discipleship is not the pursuit of self that transforms our view of God; but the pursuit of God transforms the self – our whole selves.

Matthew 16 shows us that the person of Christ cannot be separated from the work of Christ. Thus, it also shows that the way to follow the person of Christ is to carry the cross of self-denial, not the crown of seif-improvement. "For what we proclaim is not ourselves, but Jesus Christ as Lord, with ourselves as your servants for Jesus' sake." (see 2 Corinthians 4:5)

We must break away ourselves and our local churches from self-centered discipleship by being reoriented to who God is and who we are. Our local churches should completely orient themselves toward the character and nature of God. A very popularly used quote in the history of Theology is from John Calvin's *Institutes of the Christian Religion*. He begins this magnificent work with saying, "Nearly all wisdom we possess, that is to say, true and sound consists of two parts: the knowledge of God and knowledge of ourselves."[14] Discipleship is being reoriented to who God is and who we are. That God is Creator, and we are His creation:

- That He is perfect, and we are both beautiful as image-bearer and broken as sinners.
- That He is the Redeemer, and we are in need of redemption.

Sadly, many of our people have grown bored with Jesus the reason being that many church leaders have also become bored. When this happens it is indicative that we have settled for a cultural discipleship that is anemic and will not sustain the disciples of Jesus. Looking at the two biblical Christianity and cultural Christianity we find a different message portrayed:

- The message of cultural Christianity is that God is merely good to us; so we should seek God's goods.

  The message of biblical Christianity is that God is good for us; so we should seek God's goodness.

- The message of cultural Christianity is we should seek God so that He might provide for us.

---

[14] John Calvin, *Institutes of the Christian Religion, 1:35.*

The message of biblical Christianity is that God is our provision.

- The message of cultural Christianity is that we should seek God in order to get things (more stuff).

The message of biblical Christianity is that we should seek God to get the highest thing – namely Himself.

I pray that you can see the vast differences between those two theologies. The message of cultural Christianity and deep, biblical, holistic discipleship are not even close. They are at unreconcilable odds. Do you get the idea that people may be satisfied with church but bored with Jesus? Doesn't it terrify you pastor (it does me) that people may enjoy the sermon, participate in small group ministry, volunteer for whatever, and be completely satisfied by their experience – yet be apathetic toward the person and work of Christ.

## TWO COMPETING VISIONS

These two messages (visions) have real life implications for the life of discipleship in the local church. Discipleship is motivated by our beliefs about who God is. Unfortunately, the message of cultural Christianity is what is forming the majority of the people in our local churches.

# STUDY GUIDE: CHAPTER 3

1. Paul reminded the Philippian church that _____ is a reminder that we belong to Jesus.
2. In Antioch the disciples were first called _____.
3. We must put on our spiritual _____.
4. Many people think that _____ and _____ are the same.
5. People see exactly what we _____ by how we _____.
6. Explain what we mean by "died with Him on the _____ and now in Him we have _____.
7. Do you really trust God?

# CHAPTER FOUR

## Abandoned By God

*"Yet you have forsaken me and served other gods; therefore, I will save you no more. Go and cry out to the gods whom you have chosen; let them save you in the times of your distress."* (Judges 10:13, 14 ESV)

One of the most learned stories in the Old Testament concerned King Saul, the first king of Israel, when Samuel explained to him, "Because you have rejected the Word of the LORD, He has also rejected you from being king" (I Samuel 15:23). Also see Samson in Judges 16:20. Earlier in Judges 10:13-14, the Israelites experienced a similar judgment from God.

In Proverbs 1:24-31, we see a personified divine wisdom, offering this solemn warning to the one who refuses to listen:

Because I called and you refused,
I stretched out my hand and no one paid attention.
And you neglected all my counsel
and did not want my reproof.
I will also laugh at your calamity.
I will mock when your dread comes,
when your dread comes like a storm
and your calamity comes like a whirlwind,
when distress and anguish come upon you.
Then they will call on me, but I will not answer.
They will seek me diligently, but they will not find me,
because they hated knowledge
and did not choose the fear of the LORD.
They would not accept my counsel,
They spurned all my reproof.

So they shall eat of the fruit of their own way
And be satiated with their own devices.

It is apparent, those who chose to reject divine wisdom will be abandoned by God. Sadly, when that point is reached, it will be too late. They will face the dreary consequences of their foolish choices. Listen, Judges 16:20 says, "He did not know that the LORD had departed from him."

## NOT FOR INDIVIDUALS ONLY

A quick search of history will reflect that this rejection by God includes nations also. Again, in the Old Testament Israel, was abandoned by God because of unrepentant idolatry. Notice the dreadful words of Hosea 4:17, referring to Israel by the name of Ephraim: "Ephraim is joined to idols; let him alone." After the people abandoned God, He abandoned them. Jesus brought this truth out while instructing His disciples concerning His confrontations with the Pharisees (see Matthew 21:43).

Because God had rejected Israel's religious leaders, Jesus instructed His disciples to do the same: "Let them alone; they are blind guides of the blind" (Matthew 15:14). God had abandoned the nation's leadership. Observing all of this reality from Scripture is one thing – but it is quit sobering to evaluate contemporary America's church culture by it.

Lately, we hear much discussion about the Christian principles on which this nation was founded, at the same time speaking about that time in history when American society revered biblical morality. Although many in this Country are hoping and praying that God does not abandon our nation – many remain passive and fail to see that through sinful choices many in our country celebrate these choices and (seem to be laughing at God and shaking their fists at Him).

It is high time for America's pulpits to speak to this reality. Paul speaks of this kind of God's wrath working in our culture (study carefully and prayerfully Romans 1:18-32). Notice, its beginning:

*"For the wrath of God is revealed from heaven against all ungodliness and unrighteousness of men, who by their unrighteousness suppress the truth."* (v. 18 ESV)

Then, starting in verse 24, he explained in detail the clear characteristics of a society abandoned by God:

> *Therefore, God delivered them over in the desires of their hearts to sexual impurity, so that their bodies were degraded among themselves. They exchanged the truth of God for a lie, and worshipped and served what has been created instead of the Creator, who is praised forever. Amen. For this reason God delivered them over to disgraceful passions. Their women exchanged natural sexual relations for unnatural ones. The men in the same way also left natural relations with women and were inflamed in their lust for one another. Men committed shameless acts with men and received in their own persons the appropriate penalty of their error.*
>
> *And because they did not think it worthwhile to acknowledge God, God delivered them over to a corrupt mind so that they do what is not right. They are filled with all unrighteousness, evil, greed, and wickedness. They are full of envy, murder, quarrels, deceit, and malice. They are gossips, slanderers, God-haters, arrogant, proud, boastful, inventors of evil, disobedient to parents, senseless, untrustworthy, unloving, and unmerciful. Although they know God's just sentence – that those who practice such things deserve to die – they not only do them, but even applaud others who practice them.* (vv. 24-32 CSB)

Those engaging in homosexuality are not simply abandoning what is "natural," biologically speaking, they are rejecting the way God intended all of creation to operate. Paul was saying that humans are created for natural, heterosexual relationships within marriage between one man and one woman – that is the only kind of sexual relationship the Bible recognizes as acceptable. This is the context within which God greatly blesses the sexual experience. All other experiences God will judge.

# ENJOY MARRIAGE

Critics sometimes argue that passages extolling the pleasures of sex are inappropriate and should not be in the Bible. The Book of Proverbs, though, sees sex as a gift from God that is to be enjoyed in the context of the marriage commitment:

*Drink water from your own cistern,*
*water flowing from your own well.*
*Should your springs flow in the streets,*
*streams in the public square?*
*They should be for you alone*
*and not for you to share*
*with strangers.*
*Let your fountain be blessed,*
*and take pleasure in the wife*
*of your youth.*
*A loving deer, a graceful doe*
*let her breasts always satisfy you,*
*be lost in her love forever.*
*Why, my son, would you lose yourself*
*with a forbidden woman*
*or embrace a wayward woman?*
*For a man's ways are before*
*the LORD's eyes,*
*and he considers all his paths.*
*A wicked man's iniquities will trap him.*
*he will become tangled in the ropes*
*of his own sin.*
*He will die because there is no discipline,*
*and be lost because of his great stupidity.*
– Proverbs 5:15-23 CSB

An intimate relationship with one's spouse and the physical delight such a relationship can bring is commanded by the Proverbs and is seen as a powerful antidote to the temptations that can lead to unfaithfulness and immorality.

# COUNTER-CULTURAL MARRIAGE

The secular, post Christian culture quips, "Our understanding of marriage is built upon our understanding of sexuality:

According to our culture, sexual differences are merely social constructs. We know that men and women have physical distinctions, but these can be altered or disregarded, according to our preference.

Even if we do hang on to an understanding of human beings as distinctly male and female, we accept them as equal – and by equal we mean identical. Therefore, it makes complete sense for a man to marry a man or a woman to marry a woman, just as it makes sense for a man to marry a woman. There is no difference since we are identical – *so says* our secular, anti-Christian, postmodern world culture!

# BUT WHAT DOES GOD SAY?

The first two chapters of Genesis record complementary accounts of human creation. The first chapter of Genesis informs us, "God created man in His own image, in the image of God He created him; male and female He created them." (v. 27 NASB). The dignity of men and women is on display from the very beginning. Nothing else in all creation is portrayed "in the image of God, but not in the sense that we share all of His qualities:

- He is Infinite – we are finite
- He is divine – we are human
- He is Spirit – we are flesh

Therefore, in a way that nothing else in creation can, men and women share certain moral, intellectual, and relational capacities with God. We have the power to reason, the desire to love, the ability to speak, and the facility to make moral decisions. Most important of all, men and women have the opportunity to relate to God in a way that nothing else in creation can. As soon as God created man and woman, He immediately blessed them, beginning a relationship with the only beings in all the order of creation who resembles Him.

Additionally, here in the very beginning men and women are both created with equal dignity before God and each other. In this way, God speaks from the very beginning of Scripture against any kind of male or female superiority or dominance. God reinforced it near the end of Scripture, where He refers to men and women as fellow "heirs ... of the grace of life." (see I Peter 3:7)

According to God's design, men are never to be perceived as better than women, and women are never to be perceived as better than men. God hates any treatment of men or women as inferior objects. Throughout eternity no gender will be greater than the other. No one should feel superior or inferior by nature of being a man or a woman.

---

Both man and woman are equally created in the image of God.

---

Both are equally created in the image of God. But not *identically*. Right after He blesses them, He *commands them, "Be fruitful and multiply and fill the earth."* (see Genesis 1:28) This command is unique by virtue of the peculiarity of male and female. Prayerfully and carefully study chapters 1-3 of Genesis so that you might know and speak the truth into this present culturally guided end-time people, who are daily falling further from Truth and the True and Living God to embrace the false ideologies of false prophets, false teachers, false gods of religion, and other spiritualities, hedonism, secular humanism, and self-autonomy.

God's divine design for humanity involves far more than the capacity to reproduce – there is something greater than evolutionary adaptation going on. God created man and woman to cherish their shared equality while complementing their differences.

## MORE THAN A LITTLE PIECE

It has been said, we all leave a bit of ourselves behind when we move to another place. But to become a long-term resident of Villas Las Estrella, Antarctica, leaving a piece of yourself behind is a literal matter. Realizing that it could be fatal if a resident there had their appendix burst on them. The nearest hospital is 625 miles away, so every citizen must undergo an appendectomy prior to moving there.

Some would exclaim, that's requiring too much to actually leave my appendix here in order to move there. Think about what we must leave behind to become a resident of the kingdom of God.

## COUNT THE COST

Just as people are today, people in that day wanted to follow Jesus on their own terms and not His. In fact today people are so determined to have their way they are willing to deny and deconstruct the truth – but to no avail! It seems that many Christians are willing to forego their biblical worldview to accommodate a twisting of Scripture. Because of this, Jesus clearly redefines what it means to be a disciple. In Matthew 16:24-27, He said,

> *"For whoever would save his life will lose it, but whoever loses his life for My sake will find it. For what will it profit a man if he gains the whole world forfeits his soul? For the Son of Man is going to come with His angels in the glory of His Father, and then He will repay each person according to what he [or she] has done.* (ESV) Emphasis is mine.

Jesus said, "whoever wants to be My disciple must deny themselves and take up their cross and follow Me" (v. 24). This includes our willingness to let go of anything that competes with Him and His kingdom. Taking up our cross, we declare a willingness to:

- Stand under social and political oppression.
- Stand even unto death for the sake of devotion to Christ.
- Stand and truly follow Him.

This is a daily declaration and posture of following His lead as He guides us into service and sacrifice. Following Jesus means so much more than leaving a little piece of our lives behind. As the in-dwelling

Spirit of God helps us, it means giving and surrendering our whole lives – including our bodies – to Jesus alone!

## FIG LEAF RELIGION

In the third chapter of Genesis we read the tragic story of Adam and Eve. It gives us a picture of what it looks like when we try to fool God when we say we believe something but actually we really don't believe it. Here we see, they disobeyed God and immediately were aware of what they have done.

> *"Then the eyes of both of them were opened, and they knew that they were naked. And they sewed fig leaves together and made themselves coverings."* (Genesis 3:7 NKJV)

Adam and Eve knew that they had done wrong, and immediately set out to fix the situation. Why? Suddenly they recognized their nakedness, but why do they think they must do something about it? And what did they do, they weaved fig leaves together into loincloths to cover their nakedness. They knew that they disobeyed God's command – it seems they think these makeshift fig leaf aprons will fix it. This quick fix of fig leaves was thoroughly insufficient. Their pathetic attempt to cover their nakedness with what I call, "fig leaf" religion.

After God has pronounced His judgment upon them, we read: In verse 21, *"And the Lord God made tunics of skin for Adam and his wife and clothed them."* God made it clear that whatever Adam and Eve had done with their fig leaves (religion) was not nearly sufficient. So God Himself had to step-in and execute the necessary action to cover their nakedness and sin. His actions made clear the fact that animals had to die – blood must be shed. We cannot *cover up* our nakedness and cannot begin to bridge the gap our sin has created between us and God. Adam and Eve had not seen the depth of their *disobedience*.

What is your take-away from all of this? We can see in their actions the constituting of the first "religious" act in history. Adam and Eve got the idea that they might fool God through their covering themselves with fig leaves. Like so many in our churches today, who know enough for conviction, but won't repent, and humble themselves before God. Not repenting, and confessing have doubled the estrangement from Him. God nonetheless is merciful.

---

We need to take heed of their actions for our own purposes, to tell God we believe something, when we do not truly believe – [according to James in his letter] we are actually repeating the sinful actions of Adam and Eve by covering ourselves with fig leaves.

---

## DECEPTION AND A LIE

When Adam and Eve covered their nakedness and sin with fig leaves, they were lying to themselves. So when we try to fool ourselves and God – this way, our sin takes on a deeper dimension. Certainly it is one thing *not* to truly believe what commands us to believe, and to be honest about our belief. But it is something else to say we do believe and do not – then downgrade God's command to a question? Did God say? Like James says, "We have reduced His command, to a mere intellectual suggestion."

Many churches have their traditional denominational church covenants, or a statement of beliefs posted in conspicuous locations for all to see what we do along with our required standard of behavior. Thus, to say that these instruments speak for us – but once again it's an attempt to fool God with fig leaf religion. God holds us accountable for what we claim to believe and expects us to live it out. Like the Church of Ephesus at the end of the first century, we have forgotten our first love.

We have moved far from that open and honest relationship with our Lord and Savior Jesus Christ who died for our sins and loves us sacrificially. We have proven that we do not really believe these doctrines and have relegated them to intellectual assent to some words that through our life living have proven that we do not actually believe and live the words of the true Biblical doctrine as we claim.

Living out our Christian faith is less an issue of what we *believe* than an issue of in *whom we trust.* The Scripture tells us, the devil and his demons "believe" in God and hate Him. That intellectual assent so popular in churches today is insufficient and offensive to God. He is looking for everything we have to give, our whole selves.

## STUDY GUIDE: CHAPTER 4

1. One of the most learned stories is the Old Testament concerns King Saul, the first king of Israel was rejected by God because he rejected the _____ of_____.
2. Has God rejected America?
3. Both man and woman are equally create in the _____ of _____ but not identical.
4. We must be willing to let go anything that _____ with Jesus Christ and His kingdom.
5. Adam and Eve knew they had done wrong, so they immediately set out to fix the situation. Why?
6. We've moved so far from our Lord and Savior Jesus Christ, who died for our sins and _____ us sacrificially.
7. The _____ assent so popular in churches today is insufficient and offensive to God.

# SECTION TWO

# CHANGING TIMES

# CHAPTER FIVE

# Pursue Holiness

*Pursue ... holiness, without which no one will
see the Lord.* (Hebrews 12:14 NKJV)

The word "pursue" is the Greek word *"dioko,"* which is defined as *"to do something with intense effort and with definite purpose or goal."* This means "passionately" chasing after holiness with the intent to apprehend it. Our first question concerning this matter should be, "are we addressing *positional holiness or practical holiness?"*

Whatever your particular sin problem or problems may be the Bible has the answer for you. We can walk in obedience to God's Word and live a life of holiness. As we shall see in this study. God expects every born from above Christian to live a holy life:

---

Since holiness is the promised birthright of every Christian. Paul's statement, "Sin shall not be our master."

---

The biblical concept of holiness may seem a bit antiquated to our current generations. To some people the very word *holiness* means dressing in a certain way and talking a certain way. To others the idea is associated with a repugnant "holier than thou" attitude. Not only is one whole book (Leviticus) devoted to the subject, but the idea of holiness is also woven throughout the content of Scripture. More importantly, God specifically *commands* us to *be holy* (see Leviticus 11:44). As so many of God's commands, "be holy" has suffered from many who have turned it into a question. This has resulted many false concepts and forms. The lists varies depending on the group:

- To some groups holiness is equated with a list of prohibitions, such as no smoking, drinking, gambling, or dancing.
- For others it means unattainable perfection.
- Then there are those, with a dos and don'ts list.

When we follow such approaches to holiness, we are in danger of becoming like the Pharisees with their endless lists of inadequacies. All of these approaches contain some degree of accuracy, but all miss the true concept. To be holy is:

- to be morally blameless.
- to be separated from sin and therefore, consecrated to God.
- To be separated to God, and the conduct befitting those so separated.

## EXAMPLES FROM NEW TESTAMENT WRITERS

To ensure the best way of understanding the concept of holiness is through use of the word by writers of the New Testament:

1. The apostle Paul used the term in contrast to a life of immorality and impurity (see 1 Thessalonians 4:3-7).
2. The apostle Peter used the word in contrast to be living according to the evil desires we had when we lived outside of Christ (see 1 Peter 1:14-16).
3. The apostle John contrasted one who is holy with those who do wrong and are vile (see Revelation 22:11).

---

To live a holy life then, is to live a life in conformity to the moral precepts of the Bible and in contrast to the sinful ways of the world.

---

It is a life characterized by "putting off" your old self which is being corrupted by its deceitful desires ... and "putting on" the new self, created to be like God in true righteousness and holiness" (see Ephesians 22, 24).

If holiness is a command of God and so basic to the Christian life:

- Why do so few pursue it?
- Why is it so foreign to our daily living?
- Why do so many Christians feel defeated in their struggle with sin?
- Why does the Church so often seem to be more conformed to the world around it than to God?

If you had a Hebrew dictionary handy, you would find the answer. You would discover that the root concept of holiness lies in the word *separation*. Holiness has been defined by individuals and denominations in numerous different ways. However, holiness is unmistakable, and exposed in the Bible through the drama of Moses and the burning bush:

> *And Moses said, "I will turn aside and see this great sight, why the bush is not burned." When the LORD saw that he turned aside to see, God called to him out of the bush. "Moses, Moses!" And then he said, "Here am I." Then he said, "Do not come near; take your sandals off your feet, for the place on which you are standing is holy ground."* (Exodus 3:3-5 ESV)

Holy ground? How could the ground be holy? If Moses had scooped up a handful of "unholy" ground and compared it the "holy" ground at the burning bush – would he have seen the difference? No, it's the same old desert dirt, then why did the Lord declare this ground to be holy?

The ground became holy simply because God separated it as the unique place where He would reveal Himself to Moses. Meantime all the rest of the desert remains unholy because God did not choose it to be the meeting place. If God had moved one-hundred feet to the north and spoken there, that particular part of the desert would have been called holy. For example, not only did the foundational nature not change, but no one would have known the ground was holy, *unless* God revealed it to him or her.

# HOLINESS REQUIRES SEPARATION FROM AND SEPARTION TO

Holiness requires separation from one thing and separation to a different thing. Notice, you can't have one without the other! Throughout the entire Bible the root word holy and its derivatives are translated into such words as:

- Set apart
- Dedicated
- Consecrated
- Sanctified
- Holy
- Separated
- Saint

Whatever their individual context in the Bible, each is rooted in the concept of separateness. Holiness requires division. For a person to become holy in this sense, he or she must depart from anything unholy, or holiness is impossible.

Holiness requires subtraction and addition. New people, new practices, and new pursuits must be added to your life to replace the old unholy patterns. We abandon our unholy ways and pursue His holy ways. Without both aspects of this separation – biblical holiness is not possible. Again, the believer must flee from something and then follow after something else. We find these two parts in:

> *"So flee youthful passions and pursue righteousness, faith, love, and peace, along with those who call on the Lord from a pure heart."* (2 Timothy 2:22 ESV) Emphasis added.

Practical holiness for the Christian occurs when we leave behind the patterns of this world in order to become more Christlike in our character and behavior. The apostle Peter wrote:

> *But as He who called you is holy, you also be holy in your conduct, since it is written, "You shall be, for I am holy."* (1 Peter 1:15-16 ESV)

The Lord God is calling you to be holy. He calls you to come out from all conduct that is inappropriate and be separated to Him, to depart from everything that isn't like Him and devote yourself fully to Him. Holiness is the center of God's will for you. May your heart discover the incredible power of release and reattachment. May each of us depart from all that is unholy and pursue all that is holy.

## HOLINESS AND OUR WILLS

In all that has been said about our personal responsibility for holiness – the necessity of conviction and commitment, perseverance, discipline, and of holiness in body and in spirit, the activity is *always* implied:

- It is the *will* that ultimately makes each individual choice to sin or obey.
- It is the *will* that chooses to yield to temptation, or to say no.

Our *wills* then ultimately determine our moral destiny, whether we will be holy or unholy in our character and conduct. Knowing this, it is critically important that we understand how our wills operate – why they make the choices they make. Above all else, we must learn how to bring our wills under submission and obedience to the will of God, on a *practical, 24/7 basis*.

To help us understand how our wills function, a definition of the heart is necessary. In his book, *The Pursuit of Holiness,* Jerry Bridges quotes a definition which denotes all the faculties of the soul as they work together in doing good or evil – the mind, the emotions, the conscience, and the will.[15] These were implanted in the human soul by God but were all corrupted through man's fall in the Garden of Eden.

- Our understanding or reasoning was darkened (see Ephesians 4:18).
- Our desires were entangled (see Ephesians 2:3).
- Our wills were perverted (see John 5:40).

---

[15] Jerry Bridges, *The Pursuit of Holiness* (NavPress, Colorado Springs, CO 80935, 1978, 1996) page 124

When we are "born again from above," our reason is again enlightened, our affections and desires are redirected, and our wills are under submission. Although this is true, in actuality we experience it as a maturing process over time as we are:

## Being transformed by Renewing Our mind (see Romans 12:2)

People often say, "I am willing to die for Jesus." That is very honorable but let me say that God does not necessarily want you and me to die for Jesus in this Dispensation of Grace. He wants us to live for Jesus, He wants us to be *"a living sacrifice."* He wants us to be holy, and whatever we do, whether we eat, or drink, or whatsoever we do – God wants us to do it for His glory (see 1 Corinthians 10:31 KJV).

Remember Paul's dying testimony contains the statement. "I have fought a good fight. I have finished my course; I have kept the faith." (II Timothy 4:7 KJV). We are commanded to be transformed (in "the inner man"). This spiritual miracle can only happen *"by the renewing of your mind."* The Greek word used for *"renewing"* occurs but one more time in the New Testament and there in connection with *"regeneration."* In Titus 3:5 we read: *"Not by works of righteousness which we have done, but according to His mercy He saved us, by the washing of regeneration and <u>renewing</u> of the Holy Ghost."* KJV

This miracle of renewing is the work of the Holy Spirit. No person can renew him or herself in the spiritual sense. He or she can reform and try to make themselves new, but the old nature will eventually take over again. The *renewing of the mind* comes about only when we surrender our spirit, soul, and body unto God. *"... that ye may prove what is that good, and acceptable, and perfect will of God."* (KJV). This means that we may be able to discern, or recognize, the perfect will of God for our life.

## Set your Affections on Things Above (see Colossians 3:2)

When God calls you to a task, He always equips you with the abilities to accomplish His will. Do you ever worry about not having the "right credentials" needed to share Christ with someone? Listen to this story:

A speaker was presenting Christ to a large audience on one of the great university campuses. One of the professors in the audience was stricken by the power of the message and the calm and peaceful appearance of the speaker. Leaving the auditorium the professor said to a fellow professor walking beside him, "I suppose that preacher spends most of his time in study and preparation of sermons, away from the tension and strain of this busy world of ours."

*"Would you like to meet the speaker?"* the fellow professor asked. *"I know him well."* The professor said he would, so a meeting was scheduled for lunch the next day.

How shocked the professor was when he was taken to a snack room in one of the local factories. Sitting there at the table with the speaker, he asked the speaker about his profession. *"My occupation is to do the will of God and love people while I wait for Christ to return to earth,"* the speaker replied. *Meanwhile I operate one of the machines here at the factory."[16]*

The point is this: a person does not have to be a great preacher to be in the will of God. Your profession is to do the will of God and to be a strong witness for Christ no matter where God places you. Seek those things above (in heaven).

## WE MUST SUBMIT OUR WILLS TO GOD (see James 4:7)

Until we do recognize the perfect will of God for our life. We can never enjoy our spiritual birthright, which is abundant life. If we hope to see the blessings of God, we must live daily, fully surrendered to God's will. Note Paul's example, what he did was "by the will of God"; that is, his profession and work were exactly what God wanted him to do. Paul did not dare to choose his life's work without the direction of God; for he could make a mistake, and he did not want to waste his life.

He did not want to come to the end of his life and be counted a failure by God. To Paul there was only one work or profession for him: the job God wanted him to do. The profession he wanted did

---

[16] Walter B. Knight. *Knight's Treasury of 2,000 Illustrations* (Grand Rapids, MI: Eerdmans's Publishing Company, 1963), p. 34

not matter, only God's will for his life mattered. We must let Jesus sit on the throne of our heart and control every minute detail of our life.

However, when God originally created man, the *mind*, the *emotions*, and the *will* all work in perfect harmony. The mind led the way in understanding the will, the will consent to God's will and the emotions delighted in doing it. But when sin entered man's soul, these three were entangled crossing-up each other. *"Submit yourselves therefore to God. Resist the devil, and he will flee from you."* (James 4:7 ESV)

## THE UNSURRENDERED SOUL

Can anything be sweeter than being in perfect agreement with whatever God wants for you, from you, and through you? If we know this would be so good, why, do so many Christians find themselves in constant conflict over doing so? Because they are still in the first stage of *transformation* out of their "old" creatures' past into their new creatures' life. Our "old" creatures seem to exist in a time warp of our pasts. Our "now" creatures struggle to keep from stumbling and falling off the path while trying to learn how to do this "walking in the Spirit" we are (all) supposed to do. And our "new" creatures' life often seems beyond our reach – somewhere. Yet the Word of God says,

> *"Therefore, if anyone is in Christ, he [or she] is a new creation; old things have passed away; behold, all things have become new."* (2 Corinthians 5:17 NKJV) Bracket is mine.

While many Christians realize there is a transformation from the old creature to the new creature that has to happen – and that a doable process of change me takes place. This *struggle* with this *old-to-new* transformation is not a new problem of these times – it has always been around since the fall of Adam and Eve in the Garden of Eden. The Apostle Paul struggled mightily with this same conflict of moving out of the old into the new. He was already faithfully serving God with signs and wonders following him, but made himself very transparent when he admitted his struggles:

*"What I don't understand about myself is that I decide one way, but then I act another, doing things I absolutely despise. I obviously need help! I realize that I don't have what it takes. I can will it, but I can't do it. I decided to do good, but I don't really do it; I decided not to do bad, but then I do it anyway. My decisions, such as they are, don't result into actions ... I truly delight in God's commands, but it's pretty obvious that not all of me joins in that delight. Parts of me covertly rebel, and just when I least expect it, they take charge."* (Romans 7:15-24, The Message)

While the battle was greatly distressing to Paul, he did not do what many of us seem to do today – when they feel defeated. He did not become discouraged or disheartened; he did not try to justify or rationalize his problem, nor did he seek sympathy with it. He knew that Jesus Christ was the answer to this dilemma, so he just kept pressing on towards knowing Him better to end his dilemma. We must overcome our souls' self-declared war to get them lined up with our born-again spirits' knowledge of that fact! Paul said to the Philippian *believers:*

*"Wherefore, my beloved, as ye have always obeyed, not as in my presence only, but now much more in my absence, work out your own salvation with fear and trembling."* (Philippians 2:12, KJV)

Paul was admonishing believers, people whose spirits were already saved – people who had been born again. Paul told them there still was a working-out needed and it was a serious thing. It was to be done with fear and trembling. It was the salvation of their unsurrendered souls.

If your unsurrendered soul is not challenged and made to surrender, it will end up attracting unwanted old allies to aid it in its war against your born-again spirit. Unless conquered, this war will give the devil access to toss his evil weaponry – soulish rebellion and resistance from within, and demonic harassment from without. Satan knew you before you were saved, so he knows your weak spots, your old weaknesses. The Word of God proclaims through Paul's instructions to the Christians in Rome that there is freedom promised we can trust – we simply need to speak in agreement with it:

> *"The word is near you; it is in your mouth and in your heart, that is, the word of faith we are proclaiming: That if you confess with your mouth, 'Jesus is Lord,' and believe in your heart that God raised Him from the dead, you will be saved. For it is with your heart that you believe and are justified, and it is with your mouth that you confess and are saved. As the Scripture says, 'Anyone who trusts in Him will never be put to shame.'"* (Romans 10:8-11 NIV)

If you have confessed this, then your Lord and Savior, Jesus Christ is ready to live His life through you. He will flood His love, peace, and power through you.

## SOUL POWER CONTROL

God has created leadership structures within the social structures of humankind. He has instituted certain positions of authority in the home, in the church, and in the government. But human authority is *always* horizontal – it is *never* vertical. No leader's authority over you should ever take away your right to hear from God in your own spirit, which then conveys the spiritual information to your soul. It is very important that each of us realize that our very own spirit's success at actually getting the information through to our mind, will, and emotions depends upon how *surrendered* your soul is.

## SIN – A PSYCHOLOGICAL REALITY

The condition of normal human life is one where the inner resources of the person are weakened or dead, and where the factors of human life do not interrelate as they were intended by their nature and function to do. This is sin in the singular: not an act but a condition.

It is not that we are wrong, but that the inner components are no longer properly hooked up. The wires are crossed – we are twisted. Our thinking, our feeling, our very bodily dispositions are defective and connected wrongly with reference to life as a whole.

All of this comes together in the *will*. The will stands in the shambles of the human system, flailing about in effectual and sporadic jerks or driven into complete passivity. The apostle Paul gives us a definitive language for our condition before broken and corrupted soul:

> *"And you He made alive, who were dead in trespasses and sins, in which you once walked according to the course of this world, according to the prince of the power of the air, the spirit who now works in the sons of disobedience, among whom also we all once conducted ourselves in the lusts of our flesh, fulfilling the desires of the flesh and of the mind, and were by nature children of wrath, just as the others."* (Ephesians 2:1 NKJV)
>
> *"For the good that I will do, I do not do, but the evil I will not do, that I practice"* (Romans 7:19 NKJV)

We probably experienced this at some point; in fact no human being escapes the blight of the will to a certain degree, and in some it becomes a matter of dysfunctionality and misery, no longer rebellion but sickness. The person is effectively turned away from his or her own good. He or she may and often does wish to be good and to do what is right, but this person is *prepared*, is *set*, to do evil. It is what the individual is ready to do without thinking.

In this condition, the mind is confused, ignorant, and misguided. Emotions are simultaneously dominant in personality and in conflict with one another. The body and the social environment are filled with regular patterns of wrongdoing and are constantly inclined toward doing what is wrong. In this condition, the intellect finds reasons why what is bad is good (or at least not bad) and what is good is bad (or at least not good).

Once again, Paul has the appropriate description of the situation. In Romans 1:28-32, we find one of the most extensive lists of sins in Scripture. The list shows the extensive sweep of human moral depravity (compare *all* in verse 29). Note that while society tends to rationalize certain sins, God judges all sin. These sins particularly reveal our rebellious hearts. All without exception deserves God's punishment.

Paul declares that all unrighteous people are without excuse. Now he demonstrates that the self-righteous (those who judge others) are inexcusable, by revealing the standards by which everyone will be judged. Judgment will be:

1. According to truth (vv. 1-5)
2. According to works (vv. 6-11)
3. According to the light one has of God's law.

Our culture (the people) having departed from godliness and righteousness, are people who suppress the truth about God. He is their loving Creator and deserves their worship and praise. Sinful people can mentally perceive the revealed truth of God (see vv. 19, 20), but they have chosen to suppress it. They are without excuse. God's anger is being revealed (the present tense) against sin and the suppression of the truth. From the intricate design of the human cell to the majesty of the Rocky Mountains, all of God's work testify to His wisdom and power.

# STUDY GUIDE: CHAPTER 5

1. God expects every born from above Christian to walk in obedience to His commands and live a life of holiness.
2. _____ _____ is the promised birthright of _____ _____.
3. God commands us to be holy (see Leviticus 11:44).
4. Holiness means to be separated to God, and conduct befitting those so separated.
5. If holiness is a command of God and so basic – why do so many question it?
6. Holiness is unmistakable and exposed in the Bible through the drama of Moses and the burning bush (see Exodus 3:3-5).
7. Our people (culture) have decided to suppress the revealed truth of God (see Romans 7:19-20).

# CHAPTER SIX

## Obedience And Surrender

*"As the Father has loved Me, so have I loved you. Now remain in My love. If you obey My commands, you will remain in My love, just as I have obeyed My Father's commands and remain in His love. I have told you this so that My joy may be in you and your joy may be complete ... You did not choose Me, but I chose you and appointed you to go and bear fruit ... fruit that will last. Then the Father will give you whatever you ask in My name."* (John 15:9-11, 16, NIV)

These verses tell us that if we obey His *commands,* we will remain in His love. Another verse says He knows that we love Him when we obey His commands. Here, Our Lord places a great deal of importance upon the act of obedience. Obedience does not always mean that you won't ever feel conflicted about what you know you must do.

Obedience does not mean you will never feel uneasy, frustrated, and at times overwhelmed. Obedience means that you will simply do what you know you should do. That is why it so important that we have our souls cleansed of all misconceptions and preconceived ideas about God's plans. You will not be overwhelmed or sidelined by your human emotions, and you will respond to your spirit's desire to do the will of God.

## O MY SOUL

In understanding the function and operation of the "soul" one can compare it to the computer at the center of a computerized production system say of a clothes washer. It is like the timer, a distinct entity. It has an inherent nature (parts) that allows it to coordinate the various activities in the system as a whole. Its own ability to function depends upon it being appropriately positioned in the larger whole.

Of course, the timer is a strictly physical entity, whereas the *soul* is not. But then, the whole that it runs is also a physical entity, as the person is not – even though the human person has essential physical components in his or her life. Granting many similarities, it is helpful to think of the soul as the "computer" that operates all dimensions of the human system by governing and coordinating what goes on in them. It has its own nature, parts, properties, and internal and external relations, as indicated earlier.

It is this sense of a deeper level of the self that accounts for characteristic "language of the soul found in the Bible and elsewhere. Note this example, the soul is typically *addressed,* or it may be referred to in the third person, by the person whose soul it is. It is treated as if it had, in some measure, a life of its own. And as a matter of fact it does. Thus:

*"Why are you, O my soul … hope in God"* (Psalm 42:5);
"Bless the Lord, O my soul" (Psalm 103:1);
"My soul keeps your decrees" (Psalm 119:167);
"My soul magnifies the Lord" (Luke 1:47).

One reason why the book of Psalms has such a powerful effect on us is that it is a "soul book." It touches at the deepest levels of our lives – far beyond our conscious thoughts and endeavors. It expresses and helps us to express the profound parts of our lives. This element of depth and distance is a primary characterization of the soul. It is of the very nature of the soul.

Along with the soul, the person is saved of course. Thus, when the Psalmist says, *"My soul is among the lions"* (Psalm 57:4), he means he is among the lions. And when the writer of Hebrews speaks of the *"saving of the soul"* (Hebrews 10:39), he means the saving of the person. With the soul, everything else comes along. But still, the person is not identical with his soul. There is much more to the person other than the soul, and in this lies hope for the restructuring of the broken and corrupted soul.

## THE RELUCTANT DISCIPLE

In the Book of Acts, we find the story about a reluctant disciple named Ananias, who actually was afraid to obey God:

> *"In Damascus there was a disciple named Ananias. The Lord called to him in a vision. 'Ananias!' 'Yes Lord,' he answered. The Lord told him, go to the house of Judas on Straight Street and ask him for a man from Tarsus named Saul, for he is praying. In a vision he has seen a man named Anaias come and place his hands on him to restore his sight,' 'Lord,' Ananias answered, 'I have heard many reports about the man and all the harm he has done to your saints in Jerusalem. And he has come here with authority from the chief priests to arrest all who call on your name.' But the Lord said to Ananias, 'Go! This man is My chosen instrument to carry My name before the Gentiles and their kings and the people of Israel. I will show him how much he must suffer for My name.' Then Ananias went to the house and entered it. Placing his hands on Saul, he said, 'Brother Saul, the Lord Jesus, who appeared to you on the road as you were coming here – has sent me so that you may see again and be filled with the Holy Spirit.' Immediately, something like scales fell from Saul's eyes, and he could see again. He got up and was baptized, and after taking food, he regained his strength."* (Acts 9:10-19 NIV)

Ananias was afraid of the task that Jesus had assigned to him. He nervously reminded Jesus of just who Saul of Tarsus was and what he was doing to the believers wherever they may be found. Don't we sometimes like Ananias, feel that the Lord may be out of touch with our reality? So we anxiously attempt to remind Him of what we've been through or presently going through.

Jesus reassured Ananias that Saul was now a believer by telling him that Saul could be found in certain house praying. Just a few days prior, Saul had been breathing out slaughter against those who would follow Jesus Christ. A Christian has no rights that are in conflict with the Word of God. While we may have a natural desire to want attention paid to our negative emotions such as fear, God is more interested in what is right for everyone involved in the situation.

> *"Do everything readily and cheerfully – no bickering, no second-guessing allowed! Go out into the world uncorrupted, a breath of fresh air in this squalid and polluted society. Provide people with a glimpse of good living and of the living God."* (Philippians 2:14-15, The Message)

Some people tend to believe that God's will is multiple choice. I have tried to convince God of this, myself and I've heard other do this too. God, this is how I see the problem. Well I can settle for (A) or (B) I suppose I could accept (C). I'm sure we're in agreement here. Which one is your will? I think God's answer is (D) *None of the above.* In Isaiah 55:8-11, God says,

> *"For My thoughts are not your thoughts, neither are your ways, my ways, saith the Lord. For as the heavens are higher than the earth, so are My ways higher than your ways, and My thoughts than your thoughts. For as the rain cometh down, and the snow from heaven, and returneth not thither, but watereth the earth, and maketh it bring and, that it may give seed to the sower and bread to the eater: so shall my word be that goeth out of my mouth; and it shall not return unto me void, but it shall accomplish that which I please, and it shall prosper into the thing whereto I send it."* KJV

We need to obey God's Word, doing what He wants rather than believing the interpretations of His Word that our souls spin. When God tells us *not* to do something – we need to just *not* do it. Sadly, we try to figure out how to reinterpret His meaning, so we are more comfortable with it. "God told me to stop watching so much TV, but do you think He meant video, and DVDs, too?"

# OBEY! – WHERE DO I START?

You start with believing that you are a part of the Bride of Christ. As part of the bride, the family of God, you are known for your "love for one another." So begin the journey of obedience by seeking to know and understand the love of God poured out upon all of His children (see Romans 5:5).

The *Message* translates Jesus' words in John 14:15, *"If you love Me, show it by doing what I've told you."* It is noticeably clear that Jesus is saying that the proof of our true love for Him is not in words – but in obedience to what He has commanded us to do. Obedience is the *fruit of our love towards Christ.* If we are not obeying what He has commanded us to do – then we are not showing the fruit of love.

It is thought that Rev. Billy Graham has preached the gospel in person to over two hundred million people. This does not include the tens of millions who read his books, magazines, and newspaper articles; watched him on television and film; and heard his messages by radio. An unknown number of people came to faith in Jesus Christ as a result of his commitment to his Savior and his pursuit of the call of God on his life. In the months before the pivotal LA revival Rev. Graham experienced an ordeal with a fellow Evangelist and friend, Charles Templeton who had walked away from his faith due to his belief that the Bible could not be trusted. The event shook Graham to his core and pushed him to a moment of decision. Years later in his autobiography, Graham recounted the night he was walking through the woods at a retreat center. Finally stopping and getting on his knees, and laid his Bible on a tree stump in front of him and launched into a prayer that would define his life and ministry:

O God! There are many things in this book I do not understand.
There are many problems with it for which I have no solution.
There are many seeming contradictions. There are some
areas in it that do not seem to correlate with modern science
I can't answer some of the philosophical and psychological
questions Chuck and some others are raising.[17]

---

[17]  Billy Graham, *Just As I Am* New York: Harper Collins, 1997), 135.

Unloading his anxieties and fears to God, Graham eventually concluded:

Father, I am going to accept this as Thy Word – by faith! I'm going to allow faith to go beyond my intellectual questions. and doubts, and I will believe this to be Your Inspired Word.[18]

In his own words, Graham crossed a major threshold from fear to faith, submitting his worldview to divine revelation over his own understanding. The purpose of this book is to challenge Christians to be servants of our Lord and Savior, Jesus Christ who shines the light of the gospel of grace in this age gone wild – as Billy Graham did so humbly and successfully.

Christians of every denomination, tradition, and community are trying to figure out how to engage this age gone wild. Yet, in Evangelist Graham's story, we see a simple *truth* that is the beginning for Christians who want to bring their best to this dark world.

---

Truth does not exist just in words – truth must have corresponding actions to verify that it is present.

---

The Father has made it quite clear that the action of truth is *"trustworthy, straightforward correspondence between deeds and words"* (Isaiah 45:19, *Amplified Bible*). Truth has a straightforward relationship with our actions and what we say. Upon hearing Jesus's reasoning together with some Pharisees, Herodians, and Sadducees, one scribe asked Jesus what the first commandment of all was. Jesus answered him:

> *"The first of all the commandment is: 'Hear, O Israel, the LORD our God, the LORD is one. And you shall love the LORD your God with all your heart, with all your soul, with all your mind, and with all your strength.' This is the first commandment. And second, like it, is true: You shall love you neighbor as yourself.' There is no other commandment greater than these."* (Mark 12:29-32, NKJV)

---

[18] Ibid.

## MAKING RIGHT CHOICES

Normally following a great loss of life from speeding car crashes, or someone loses their life through suicide, "Why didn't God stop the people from making those choices?" How would that person or persons feel if God suddenly said to them, *"You will no longer have any choices. You will stop what you are doing, and you will do what I say or else!"*

Forcing people to make right choices is not how God has set up for His New Covenant saints. I believe that just as the grumbling, mumbling, children of Israel stumbled around the desert all those years, many of us take years to walk out of our deserts also. God keeps putting obstacles in our wrong paths and keep pushing us toward right doors and opportunities.

Imagine you walked into a restaurant and ordered a steak. Twenty minutes later, the waiter returns with a plate of meatballs and spaghetti. Needless to say, you would not be happy. You would send it back because it was not what you ordered. *It is not even close!*

I feel like that is what we have done to the church. God gave us His commands for the Church. He told us precisely what He wanted through His commands in the Bible. We have very arrogantly asked questions of choice; that we think works better for us. Rather than accurately studying His commands and delivering exactly what He wants.

We have been *influenced* by so many other things. We think about what we want and what others want and are doing. In the spirit of Cain, we bring an offering that we think He should accept – rather than what He actually asked for. *It is not even close!*

---

The Holy Spirit helps us through obedience to God's Word, so that more Christlike behavior follows, and our feelings and desires aligns more with God's will.

---

# COMMANDS VERSUS QUESTIONS

I read about a little exercise that I think is very timely today to consider for church leaders. First, they are to list all the things that people are to expect from their church. Just today, October 17, 2023, I was told of a local pastor who did not believe in the church decorating and celebrating Halloween. He was fired because he would not let the church decorate the building and grounds for the upcoming event. Normally the list is of obvious things:

- A really good service
- Strong age-specific ministries
- A certain style/volume/length of singing
- A well-communicated sermon
- Conveniences such as parking
- A clean church building
- Coffee and doughnuts
- Childcare

Secondly, ask them to list the commands the Lord gave the church in Scripture. Usually the list goes:

- "Love one another as I have loved you" (see John 15:12).
- "Visit the orphans and widows in their afflictions (see James 1:27).
- "Make disciples of all nations" (see Matthew 28:19).
- "Bare one another's burdens" (see Galatians 6:2).
- "Preach the Gospel to all creation" (see Mark 16:15).

Then ask them what would upset their people the most --- if the church didn't provide the things from the first list or if the church didn't obey the commands in the second list.

In Luke 12, Jesus told a parable about a master leaving his servants with specific tasks. When the master returned, he expected to see the tasks accomplished. When he saw his *commands* neglected, the servants were severely punished. How can we shrug our shoulders at a parable like that? That is the question!

Jesus is coming back soon, and He expects to find His Church taking His *commands* seriously. Yet more often than not we are more concerned with how well the sermon was communicated, whether the youth group is relevant enough, or how to make the music better.

## What Changes the Command to a Question?

- Is it disobedience toward commands from God?
- Or is it falling short of the expectations that we have made up?

The answers to these questions more than likely just show us whether our church exists to please God or please people – whether God is leading our church, or we are.

## DILIGENT DISCIPLES

Matthew 25:14-30 contains the parable of the talents committed to three servants, a wonderful story of ministers who were aware of the necessity of investing their *spiritual gifts* in others.

> *"It's also like a man going off on an extended trip. He called his servants together and delegated responsibilities. To one he gave five thousand dollars, to another two thousand, to a third one thousand, depending on their abilities. Then he left. Right off, the first servant went to work and doubled his master's investment. The second did the same. But the man with the single thousand dug a hole and carefully buried his master's money.*
>
> *"After a long absence, the master of those three servants came back and settled up with them. The one given five thousand dollars showed him how he had doubled his investment. His master commended him: 'Good work! You did your job well. From now on be my partner.' The servant with the two thousand showed how he also had doubled his master's investment. His master*

70

*commended him: 'Good work! You did your job well. From now on be my partner.'*

*The servant given one thousand said, 'Master, I know you have high standards and hate careless ways, that you demand the best and make no allowances for error. I was afraid I might disappoint you, so I found a good hiding place and secured your money. Here it is, safe and sound down to the last cent.'*

*"The master was furious. 'That's a terrible way to live! It's criminal to live cautiously like that! If you knew I was after the best, why did you do less than the least? The least you could have done would have been to invest the sum with the bankers, where at least I would have gotten a little interest. Take the thousand and give it to the one who risked the most. And get rid of this "play it safe" who won't go out on a limb. Throw him into utter darkness.'"* (The Message)

In this parable, we can assume that the Master is Jesus Christ, and the servants are Christians. Jesus had always His spiritual leaders, His servants to be about their Father's business as He had been when He walked on this earth. To provide for this work of the Father's business, He prepares us and gives us resources to do what He left for us to do after He went away. He is at the Father's side interceding for us.

Everything Jesus Christ has ever done for us, taught us, and given to us relates directly to our purposes in His body while we are still here on earth. First Corinthians 12:7 tells us that all of these many spiritual gifts that are given to us by the Holy Spirit are given for this reason: *"The manifestation of the Spirit is given to each one for the profit of all."* (NKJV)

Be careful that you do not create a group of survivors who keep coming back to your meetings for a "fix." Instead, lead in a manner that might *cultivate* a group (disciples) who are passionate to do the Father's will. Survivors are not free, and they are not overcomers – they have only survived. Surviving is not winning!

The Master was going to travel far away to another country. When Jesus left planet earth to return to His Father in heaven, He made sure that everyone (of His own) had an equitable share of gifts to use until He returned. The parable actually says that the Master gave to one Christian servant five talents, another two, to another one; to every one according to his or her ability.

In the parable, two servants were both diligent and faithful. Faithfulness to our destiny as spiritual leaders *requires* that we be diligent.

---

Without diligence, our faith may never have any *action – or works.*

---

James asks and answers the following question:

> *"Do you want evidence that faith without deeds is useless? Was not our Ancestor.*
>
> *Abraham considered righteous for what he did when he offered his son Isaac on the altar? You see that his faith and actions were working together, and his faith was made complete by what he did. And the Scripture was fulfilled that says, 'Abraham believed God, and it was credited to him as righteousness,' and he was called God's friend. You see that a person is justified by what he does and not by faith alone. In the same way, was not even Rahab the prostitute considered righteous for what she did when she gave lodging to the spies and sent them off in a different direction? As the body without the spirit is dead, so faith without deeds is dead."* (James 2:20-26, NIV)

The first two servants were diligent in investing their gifts in others. Diligent means to be steady, earnest, energetic, untiring, zealous, and persistent. They had a tremendously successful servant attitude. They went forth and used or invested their gifts in helping others. A successful servant is not one who passively stands by until the Master finally gives a direct command. This is one attitude that the Body of Christ needs to get over. Amen!

# STUDY GUIDE: CHAPTER 6

1. It is important that we have our _____ cleansed of all misconceptions and preconceived ideas concerning God's plans.

2. How is the soul compared to a computer?

3. One reason the Book of Psalms has such a powerful effect on us: It is a _____ book.

4. When the writer of the Hebrews 10:39 (preserves the soul) he means the saving of the whole person.

5. To begin the journey of obedience by seeking to know and understand the _____ of _____ poured out upon all of His children. (study Romans 5:5).

6. God has given us His commands and instructions for His church – what have we done with them?

7. Christ prepares us and gives us resources to do what He left for us to do after He went away. These are Spiritual gifts given to by the Holy Spirit (see 1 Corinthians 12:7).

# CHAPTER SEVEN

## Aligning With God's Will

*"Do everything readily and cheerfully – no bickering, no second – guessing allowed! Go out into the world uncorrupted, a breath of fresh air in this squalid and polluted society. Provide people with a glimpse of good living and of the living God." (Philippians 2:14-15, The Message)*

"As I stated in an earlier chapter, some people think that God's will is multiple choice. We need to obey God's Word, doing what He wants instead of believing the interpretations of His Word that our limited souls spin.

One of the most wonderful results about setting your will to *align* with God's will is that you position yourself to receive not only guidance but divine power to accomplish His will. God is good!

- He knows our frame.
- He knows we are made of dust.
- He does not to expect us to accomplish His divine plans and purposes in our own strength (flesh).

He does, however, expect us to understand that our motives and intents must be clean and focused on Him before He will strengthen us with His power. Every time we open the Bible, we must always aim at finding some spiritual benefit, some word of love to strengthen our relationship with Christ, and some truth we have not wrapped around our heart. The Word of God is not a collection of sayings to ritualistically read each day to say you have had devotions.

---

God expects us understand that our motives and intentions must be *clean* and *focused* on Him before He will strengthen us with his power!

---

But here is an opportunity to peek inside the very heart of God, an opportunity to know Him better. Just reading the Scriptures to ready you for an intellectual agreement with your beliefs will not lead to life and light in Jesus Christ. The apostle Paul told the Roman Christians that the Word of God would bring hope, saying,

> *"For whatever things were written before were written for our learning, that we through patience and comfort of the Scriptures might have hope."* (Romans 15:4 *NKJV*)

In Ephesians 2:10, *Amplified Bible,* we read of the wonderful, glorious plans and purposes God has for us: *"For we are God's [own] handiwork [His workmanship] recreated in Christ Jesus, [born anew] that we may do those good works which God predestined [planned beforehand] for us, [taking paths which He prepared ahead of time] that we should walk in them – living the good life which He prearranged and made ready for us to live."* (Emphasis is mine throughout).

These are not works, paths, or a good life for us to embrace unto ourselves alone. These are all for the greater purpose of recognizing that we are all one body, filled with many members working together:

> *"... speaking the truth in love, (that we) may grow up in all things into Him who is the head – Christ – from whom the whole body, joined and knit together by what every joint supplies, according to the effective working by which every part does its share, causes growth of the whole body for the edifying of itself in love."* (Ephesians 4:15-16, *NKJV*)

The Apostle Paul encouraged the one he called "his son," Timothy with these words:

> *"But you must continue in the things which you have learned and been assured of, knowing from whom you have learned them, and that from childhood you have known the Holy Scriptures, which are able to make you wise for salvation through faith which is in Christ Jesus. All Scripture is given by inspiration of God, and is profitable for doctrine, for*

> *reproof, for correction, for instruction in righteousness, that the man of God may be complete, thoroughly equipped for every good work."* (2 Timothy 3:14-17, NKJV)

## SURRENDERING AND SUBMITTING TO HIS WILL

If we just had the *faith* to recognize what God wants to do and send our way if we would just get ready to receive it. It would be more exciting and incredible than anything we could imagine. When we get together pray and *agree in* faith that *God's will* be done, it is easy for others to see that God honors love, harmony, cooperation, and agreement among brethren.

In Hebrews 11, the ancient saints in this Hall of Faith were not commended for their accomplishments, nor for their talent, nor for their virtuous life. They were commended for their *faith*. Faith means trust and confidence in the grace of God toward you. Christianity is the only "religion" where the concept of mercy and grace exists [we will further discuss this in chapter 13]. All other religions are based on performance or sacrifices to satisfy or appease false gods. The God of the Taliban, in Islam requires people to send their sons to die for their "holy" wars. The God of Abraham, Isaac, and Jacob sent His own Son to die for holy peace and restoration of those who were lost to Him.

## A SUBMISSIVE WILL

What is salvation? It is none other than God saving man out of himself into Himself. Salvation has two facets: *cutting off and uniting with*. What is cut off is *self* – the uniting is with *God*. Whatever does not aim at deliverance from self and union with Him is not genuine salvation.

---

Anything which cannot save man from self and join him to God is vanity.

---

The battle whether to be saved or to perish is fought out in the will of man. Man's original Fall was due to the rebellion of his will against God's will; and so his present salvation is activated by having his volition brought into obedience to God:

- At the moment of rebirth man's will is not yet fully united, his fallen will nonetheless is lifted up through his or her acceptance of the Lord Jesus and his denial of Satan, self, and the world. By (you) believing God's Word and receiving His Spirit, (your) will is also renewed.
- After a person is born again, he or she receives a new heart and life; their will receives a new master, and they are under new management. *If* his or her will is obedient it becomes a part of the new life; *if* it resists, it turns out to be a formidable enemy to the new life.
- As we stated earlier, God intends to destroy the life of the soul, but not its function; therefore, upon being joined with the Lord in life, He moves to renew our soul with all its parts so that our soul may be one with our new life and consequently one with His will.

---

Salvation cannot be complete until man's will be united entirely with God's, neither can our union with God be complete without the joining of our will to Him.

---

## THE COMMON DENOMINATOR

The Scriptures reveals the fact that a common denominator lies behind all our sins: *the principle of disobedience.* Through Adam's disobedience we perish; through the obedience to Christ we are saved. Before, we were sons of disobedience; today God wants us to be sons of obedience.

- Disobedience means to follow one's own will.
- Obedience means to follow God's will.

77

The purpose of divine salvation is to encourage us to deny our will and be united with Him. Here lies a big mistake among Christians today. They envision spirituality to be a joyous feeling or profound knowledge. God seeks the emerging of their wills with His. *God wants your will!* If we are really united with God in His will, we shall cease at once every activity which emerges from ourselves. Once we are saved there can be no independent action:

- We are *dead* to self – but alive to God.
- We *no longer act* for Him on impulse and according to our way.
- We act solely *after* we are moved by God.
- We are set *free* from every motion of self.

Such union, in other words, signifies a change of center, a new beginning. In the past all activities focused on self and began with it; today everything is of God. He does not ask the nature of whatever we start; He simply inquires who started it. God discounts every element not yet freed from self – no matter how good it may appear to be.

---

"WHATSOEVER IS OF SELF IS REJECTED – BY GOD!"

---

# THE MIGHTY HAND OF GOD

Because many believers are saved but not absolutely yielded to God's will, He uses many ways to effect obedience. He moves His own by His Spirit and touches them with His love that they may obey Him alone, desiring nothing outside of *His will.* But often these do not produce the desired attitude in His children. God consequently must use His hand to lead them to where He desires them to be. His hand is seen primarily in the environment. God lays His hand heavily on His people to crush, to break, or to bind – that their wills may be hardened no more against Him.

The Lord is not satisfied until we are thoroughly united with Him in His will!

To achieve that end He permits many disagreeable things to come upon us. He lets us grieve, groan, and suffer. He arranges for many practical *crosses* to move back and forward across our path so that through them we may bow our heads and capitulate. Our volition is naturally exceedingly stubborn; it refuses to obey God until it is heavily disciplined.

By submitting ourselves under His mighty hand, willingly accepting His discipline, our will experiences one more cut and is once again delivered unto death. And if we continue to resist Him, greater affliction awaits us to bring us into subjection.

God purposely strips away all that is ours. All believers, after they are truly regenerated, conceive the desire of serving the will of God. Watchman Nee points out that, God puts His children through various unpleasant strippings. He causes them to lose material things:

- Health
- Fame
- Position
- Usefulness
- Joyous feeling
- Burning desire
- The presence and comfort of God[19]

He must show them that everything except His will must be denied. If it is God's will:

1. They should be willing to accept pain and suffering upon their physical bodies.
2. They must be ready to embrace dryness, darkness, and coldness if He seems pleased to treat them so.

---

[19] Watchman Nee, *The Spiritual Man Vol. 1:* Christian Fellowship Publishers, Inc. Available from the Publisher at 11515 Allecingie Parkway (Richmond Virginia 23235 www.c-f-p.com 1977) pg. 84-86

3. Christians must understand that they live on earth not for themselves but for His will.
4. Their greatest blessing, highest privilege and supreme glory lies in rejecting their corrupt volition of flesh and blood in order that they may be united with God's volition for the accomplishment of His heart's desire.
5. The gain or loss, glory or shame, joy, or pain of the created one is nothing to be concerned about.
6. Humbly be brought down.
7. This is the only way for believers to lose themselves in God!

As children of God, our desire should be to do His will. And in our most mature moments, we want to follow His will. In fact, like Jesus, we delight to do His will. And certainly, looking back, we are grateful for the way He has led us thus far; we are so amazed as we see how He guided us to where He wanted us to be. There are times, when we reach a point where we must say, "I must leave this in God's hands." That of course, is about coming to terms with what He wants rather than what I want. Following the will of God, requires faith and action, which at times call for risk and release. At every fork of the road, we need faith and action to follow where God is leading. It is a crisis of belief, a turning point, where we must decide. Which way? East or West? One or the other, but you cannot go both ways. Only one way will get you where you want to go. There are many examples of this crisis of belief in the Bible.

Jonah experienced that kind of crisis of belief when God directed him to "Go to Ninevah." Although he was a prophet of God, his prejudice and bigotry got between his will and God's will for him. Ninevah was the capital of Assyria. Jonah despised the Ninevites because they were pagans, filled with idolatry and violence. "Go and proclaim my message there," God told Jonah. God's command and the destination were clear. But Jonah still had a decision to make, obey God or not (?). Jonah hopped on a ship going in the opposite direction to Tarshish. God did not overlook his disobedience. He put a few obstacles in Jonah's way:

1. A violent storm
2. A death-defying near-death experience in the belly of a fish

And thirdly, He gave Jonah another chance. The fish vomited him out onto the land, God repeated his command, "Go to Nineveh and proclaim My message." Abraham's wife Sarah was another person who struggled with a crisis of belief. "You will have a child," God promised. Years passed, but she did not conceive. Finally, she decided to go about it another way. She told Abraham, "Go into my handmaiden, Hagar, and have the child by her." We are seeing the results of that decision played out this day, by the Jews (Issac) and Arabs (Ishmael), four thousand years later. Instead of waiting for God's plan. (?) The result of their decision was Ishmael.

---

"To get from where you are to where God is will require major adjustments," writes Henry Blackaby.

---

"These adjustments may relate to your thinking, circumstances, relationships, commitments, actions, and/or beliefs." Blackaby warns, "you cannot stay where you are and go with God at the same time."[20]

---

[20] Henry T. Blackaby and Claude V. King, *Experiencing God* (Nashville, Tenn.: Broadman & Holman Publishers, 1994), P. 38.

## STUDY GUIDE: CHAPTER 7

1. To align your will with God's will, you position yourself to receive not only _____ but _____ _____ to accomplish His will.

2. God will strengthen us with His power if our _____ and _____ are clean and focused on Him.

3. In Ephesians 2:10, we read of the wonderful, glorious _____ and _____ God has for us.

4. Salvation has two facets: a _____ _____ and a _____ _____.

5. At the moment of rebirth man's will is not yet _____ _____.

6. If we are really united with God in His will, we shall cease at once _____ _____ which emerges from ourselves.

7. After receiving true regeneration, all conceive the desire of serving the _____ of God.

# CHAPTER EIGHT

# *Where Your Treasures Are*

*"Do not store up for yourselves treasures on earth, where moth and rust destroy and where thieves, break in and steal."* (Matthew 6:19 NASB)

The loss of financial stability can and does happen for many reasons other than being cheated or making bad investments. Money has a way of getting away from us. In many places in the Bible, we are warned that money is transient as time:

- Proverbs 27:24 says that *"for riches do not last forever."*
- Through His prophet Haggai, the Lord told the backslidden Israelites that *that they were earning wages only to put the money into a bag with holes* (Haggai 1:6).
- Paul warns us not to trust in wealth, which is uncertain (1 Timothy 6:19).

In Matthew 6:19 above, Jesus was not forbidding us to be prudent savers or to plan for the future. He was simply saying our permanent wealth is eternal, but the dollar is not.

## THE BIBLE APPROACH TO MONEY

*"But if anyone does not provide for his own, and especially for those of his household, he has denied the faith and is worse than an unbeliever."* (1 Timothy 5:8)
*"Anyone who neglects to care for family members in need repudiates the faith. That's worse than refusing to believe in the first place."* (1 Timothy 5:8, The Message)

A believer is to provide for his own (his near relatives) and his household (his immediate family). Failure to care for one's family is equal to denial of the faith. Children are to obey their parents and parents are to treat their children in such a way that the children will want to obey. Children must obey their parents for Christ's sake, even if the parents are not believers. (see Ephesians 6:1-4)

This is supported by the only one of the Ten Commandments *followed by a promise* (see Deuteronomy 5:16; Ephesians 6:2). Today, too many young Americans, Gen Zers, and millennials, feel that achieving the financial stability of their parents' generation is impossible. The price of starter homes has skyrocketed. So have college loans and childcare. Meanwhile, older generations are living and working longer, limiting younger workers' chances to advance their careers and boost their salaries.

Surveys show that two-thirds of Americans believe younger people face hardships today that previous generations did not, and 65% of Gen Zers and 74% of millennials say they believe they are starting further behind financially than earlier generations at their ages.[21]

The *anxiety* around money is intense in the present days. Seventy percent of Americans say the economy is getting worse. The entire generation coming of age feels that in this fractured and divisive world – traditional systems no longer work for them.

The strength and stability of a society are related directly to the strength and stability of the authentic biblically based church.

## THE DESCENDENT PRINCIPLE

- "The rod and reproof give wisdom, but a child left to himself brings shame to his mother." (Proverbs 29:15)
- "A good man leaves an inheritance to his children's children, but the wealth of the sinner is stored up for the righteous." (Proverbs 13:22)

---

[21] Extracted from a Fayetteville Observer front page article, *For Gen Z, Millennials, the American dream feels impossible,* according to an online survey of more than 2000 U.S. adults conducted exclusively for USA TODAY by The Harris Poll on August 25-27, 2023.

- "But if anyone does not provide for his own, and especially for those of his household, he has denied the faith and is worse than an unbeliever." (1 Timothy 5:8)
- "For the children ought not to lay up for the parents, but the parents for the children." (2 Corinthians 12:14)

In his book Just *Walk Across the Room: Simple Steps Pointing People to Faith,* Bill Hybels talks about an experience that underscored the difference between the temporary (earthly) and the permanent (eternal):

I was sitting in a meeting one time when the speaker suddenly pulled out a roll of stickers. "There is something we must all understand," he said, as he walked across the front of the room. Periodically, he would stop and put a red sticker on a tiny replica of a desk-sized house, and a hot-wheeled car that represented our vocational lives.

"You may not be able to tell from where you are setting, but each red sticker has a single word on it," he said. "The word is *'temporary.'* And these things I am putting them on are all temporary. They will fade away turning cartwheels like leaves in the wind when the world ends. If you are living for these things, then you are living a life of:

- temporary pleasure
- temporary satisfaction
- temporary fulfillment

He continued to walk around the room, now silent as he labeled everything in sight with red stickers. I watched his hands declare the fate of the best this world has to offer as those stickers made their way to the goods in front of us. Temporary. Temporary. Temporary. "There is only *one* thing in this room that is not temporary," he continued. "There is only one thing that you can take with you into the next world."

He called someone up to join him on the stage, and he placed a blue sticker on her lapel. "When you get to the end of your life and take your last breath," he said, "what do you want your life to have been about?"

No earthly commodity is going to make it from this world into the next. Not land, not homes, not bank accounts, not titles, not achievements. Only *souls!*[22] Jesus Christ taught that every human being would be resurrected to spend an eternity in community with God in heaven or in isolation from God in hell. Having full knowledge of these eternal realities, He focused His attention on the only element that would extend into the next reality: people!

I don't know what the final assessment of my earthly life will be once I am gone. But I know this much: my quest while I am here to seek people out and point them toward faith in God. I've tried enough approaches in my eight decades of living to know that to invest yourself in anything other than people is to settle for the pursuit of a lesser vision – that ugly ensnaring trap of the temporal.[23]

# THE CHOICE IS YOURS

Where do you invest your time, attention, and resources? We all have resources we choose to invest, whether it be possessions and finances or intangibles like time, attention, thoughts, or prayers. Therefore, some decisions lead to blessings; and others, to loss. Can you recall a misplaced investment that caused you such a loss and how experiencing it made you feel?

In Matthew 6:20, Christ instructs us to store up "treasures in heaven" instead. What would it be like to give your time to something connected to heaven and its rewards? To give your attention? Thoughts? Prayers? Possessions and finances? To move from earthly to heavenly investing, we must change our desires. In (v. 21), Jesus says our hearts will follow our treasure.

That means we can change our desires by changing where we place our resources. For example, if you pray for an enemy, God will increase your concern for that person.

---

Storing treasure in heaven is the most wise and worthwhile thing we can do with treasures on earth.

---

[22] Adopted from *The Coming Economic Armageddon* by Dr. David Jeremiah (Faith Word Hachette Book Group New York, NY 2010) pages 241-242

[23] Bill Hybels, *Just Walk across the Room: Simple Steps Pointing people to Faith* (Grand Rapids: Zondervan, 2006), 186-187.

Throughout Scripture, God urges us to use what we have to receive spiritual rewards. And in Jesus there are only benefits for such a choice. We know that to overcome clinging to temporal things – take effort but in eternity we will be eternally glad that we did.

# STUDY GUIDE: CHAPTER 8

1. Children must obey their parents for
   _____ _____.

2. The anxiety around _____ is very intense today.

3. The strength and stability of a _____ are related directly to the _____, and _____ of the authentic biblically based church.

4. "A good man leaves a _____ to his children's children – but – the wealth of a sinner is stored up for the _____."

5. There is only one thing that you can take with you into the next world, _____.

6. Christ taught that every human being would be resurrected to spend eternity in community with God _____ _____ or in isolation from God in _____.

7. To invest yourself in anything other than _____ is to settle for the _____ of a lesser vision – the temporal.

# SECTION THREE

# GOD ALWAYS VALUES
# FAITHFUL SERVICE

# CHAPTER NINE

## Making Whole Disciples

*"… until Christ is formed in you"*
Galatians 4:19

While the initiative in the transformation process of the soul initially comes from God above by the Holy Spirit, we are never to merely sit passively at any point in the process. *God created all of us to be discipled!* This is clear from the biblical imperatives repent, believe in new life in Jesus Christ and have faith in His death (shed blood), and His resurrection. Having died with Him by faith now we have new life. We must put off the old person and put on the new, to work out the salvation given to us. Jesus made it clear, "apart from Me you can do nothing" (see John 15:5).

Therefore, the invasion of the personality by new life from above does not in itself *form* the personality in the likeness of Christ. It does not of itself restore the soul into the wholeness intended for its creation. Alone it does not bring one to the point where "the things I would, that I do, and the things I would not, I do not," where "sin will have no dominion over you" (see Romans 6:14). Rather, I must learn and accept the *responsibility* of moving *with* God in the transformation of my own personality.

Intelligent and steady implementation of plans for change are required if I am to lose the incoherence of the broken soul and take on the easy obedience and fulfillment of the person who lives ever more fully within the Kingdom of God and the friendship of Jesus.

# PROGESS IN WHOLENESS

How do *I* go about doing my part in the process of my own transformation? The answer to this question is the practice of spiritual disciplines. I call them your "holy habits" and "one another ministries" for the spiritual life. They refer to what we must do. What is a discipline?[24] A discipline is an activity within our power, something we can do that brings us to a point where we can do what we at present cannot do by direct effort. This principle of discipline is even more important in the *spiritual life*. The Spirit and the Word working in tandem are our standard and guide. Discipline is in fact a natural part of the structure of education, culture, or no other attainments are achieved without it. While much discipline i.e., spankings and other means are for behavioral programs. While this is a great point. Spiritual disciplines are not primarily for the solving of behavioral problems, although that is one of the effects. For example, many of our various rehab programs focus on things we can do. We can attend meetings, openly own up in public, or call on others in the group in time of need, but (can he or she) stay sober?

The aim of disciplines in the spiritual life – and, specifically, in following Christ is the transformation of the total state of the soul. It is the renewal of the whole person from the inside out, involving differences in thought, feeling, and character that may never be manifest in outward behavior at all. This is what Paul has in mind when he speaks of *"and have put on the new self, which is **being renewed** to a knowledge according to the image of the One who created it"* (Colossians 3:10 NASB).

The gist of the moral teachings of Jesus and his first students was his insistence that you cannot keep the law by trying not to break the law. Instead, you have to be *transformed* in the functions of the soul so that the deeds of the law are a natural outflow of who you have become. This is spiritual formation in the Christian sense, and it

---

[24] https: en.wipkedia.org/wiki/ accessed 10/12/23. Discipline is an action or nonaction that is regulated to be in accordance with a particular system of governance. All the ways we guide our children toward discipleship with our words and action.

must *always* be kept in mind when we consider Jesus's teachings about various behaviors in the Sermon on the Mount and elsewhere.

His teaching concerning turning the other cheek, for example:

- If your intentions are to just do it – you will notice you can do that with your heart full of bitterness and malice.
- However, if you become a person who has the character of Christ on the inside, automatically you would do so without thinking about it.

Discipline is by no means all that is involved. In fact, they do not take the place, and they cannot be effective without, the word of the gospel along with the movements of the Holy Spirit in our lives. However, the Spirit nor the gospel will not *take* their place. Some people are unable to put them into practice. Such people need help and ministry suitable to the particular case and circumstances. But people who are not totally shattered, and who have experienced the birth from above, can usually, with simple instruction and encouragement, begin to make real progress toward *wholeness* by persistent practices such as:

- Prayer
- Solitude
- Silence
- Fasting
- Daily Bible reading
- Scripture memorization
- Corporate and Individual praise and worship, etc.

The various disciplines minister to different and complementary aspects of our brokenness. Positively, we learn that God meets our needs in His own ways. The first freedom we have is always the choice of where we will place our minds. That freedom is enhanced by the freedom to study and fill our minds with the Word of God. In study our mind takes on the order in the object studied, and the life arising out of it. It is sad how little of the Bible is known by heart by people who claim to honor it. When Jesus included in His Commission *"teaching them everything I have commanded,"* underscoring the fact that a disciple is first of all *a learner*. This is why the early church gathered regularly for "the apostles' teaching" (see Acts 2:42). It is why the ancient church established catechetical long instructions in Christian doctrine and practice.

## SPIRITUAL LIFE

The Great Commission is God's plan for lifelong learners, who have pastors and teachers who care enough to bring them to even greater maturity in Christ. Believers need to be immersed in the gospel every week. They also need to learn God's commands *for grateful living* in view of His mercies. This can only be accomplished through consistent, loving, patient, and in-depth teaching. Baptism is not just a ritual that we administer at the beginning of the Christian life; it is God's public act of claiming us (we died and rose to new life in Him). *Everything* in Scripture is given for our instruction!

Paul's exhorts even learned Timothy to recall "what you have learned and have firmly believed" through the catechesis of his mother and grandmother, "and how from childhood you have been acquainted with the sacred writings, which are able to make you wise for salvation through faith in Christ Jesus" (2 Timothy 3:14-15 ESV). He adds, "All Scripture is breathed out by God and profitable for teaching, for reproof, for correction, and for training in righteousness, that the man of God may be competent, equipped for every good work" (2 Timothy 3:16-17 ESV).

## PREACH THE WORD!

Next, Paul charges Timothy to "Preach the Word" (4:2). Paul wanted to make sure that Timothy preached the Word without *mixture*. The Bible is the only divinely authorized record of the divine love of God and of what God's love has done (and is doing) for those who put their faith and trust in His Son. The Bible is the only book that tells us that because of God's love, Christ Jesus met and paid the sin debt by which His death purchased redemption, paid the ransom, and took our sins away, bearing them in His own body on the cross (see 1 Peter 2:24).

The Bible is the only book that tells us that in the beginning, before God made either the earth or man. He planned and perfected our salvation (see 1 Peter 1:20). It is the only authentic revelation of God and His only begotten Son; It is the only book that tells us that it is not God's will that any should perish, but that all should come to *repentance*. The Bible declares its inspiration; it is the only book on earth that is *a living book*. The message God wants all people to hear is laid down in His Word.

Paul was burdened. He was facing death; and knowing that his departure was near, and the urgency of preaching the gospel weighted very heavily on his heart. He wanted Timothy to announce the second coming of the Lord Jesus Christ, so clearly outlined in 1 Thessalonians 4:13-18: warn of judgment; the judgment of everyone for stewardship; and at the consummation of all things, the judgment of the wicked. Christians will not be judged after death as to whether they are saved or lost; they will be judged only for stewardship. Carefully study: II Corinthians 5:10 and I Corinthians 3:11-15.

Paul also had the kingdom in mind. There will be a kingdom, and Jesus will be King. Paul wanted Timothy to surrender all of his ability, energy, strength, and resources to the preaching of these fundamentals of the faith. In patience, love, faith, and longsuffering (and in the face of prejudiced opposition by the enemies of the Gospel) he should preach God's message to a dying world.

Timothy was to cry aloud concerning the judgment; he was announcing the coming kingdom. He was to reprove believers, when necessary, rebuke the unconcerned, exhort the spiritually-minded to higher things – and he was to do this with long-suffering.

# DISCIPLESHIP IN THE HOME

For some reason, the mission field to most Americans is always somewhere overseas. Is it too late for us to conclude that our nearest mission field is our own family? In his Pentecost sermon, Peter declared, "The promise is for you and *for your children* and for all who are far off, everyone whom the Lord our God calls to Himself" (Acts 2:39 ESV). So, the Great Commission is *a call* not only to foreign missions and church planting but to the succession of *covenant blessings* from one generation to the next.

Everyone who is "born again" from above is a visible member of the family, and this means that every one of us is not only privileged but responsible to learn the language and to live it out among the saints and in the world. No believer can say that learning and growing in the Christian faith and practice is an optional extra. Too busy climbing the professional ladder? "We have been bought with a price, not with money but with the precious blood of Jesus Christ" (see 1 Peter 1:18-19).

Are we too engaged with entertainment, sports, and other cultural pursuits to shepherd Christ's little flock in your home? Is the pace of "family life" so all-consuming that we have no time for God's grace? If so, we should not be surprised if one day our children are not a part of the body of Christ, the Church of Jesus Christ.

How do you get a child to obey and follow you? Parents have a choice either to threaten a child or train a child to follow willingly. Unfortunately, many of us find it easier to threaten our children to obey. For example, let us take a look at the school's ballfield as the youngsters practice for the big game.

*"If you don't pay attention to the game, I'm going to jerk you off the field!"* shouted the coach. He was a pretty intense person who hated to lose. In fact, he refused to lose. His philosophy in life was pretty simple: drive people into the ground by yelling at them. Name -calling was a valid part of the menu.

During one of these intense practices, seven-year-old Andrew could not take it anymore. He was doing the best he could, he really was, but it was not enough to please the coach. *"Be a leader or get out of the way!"* the coach yelled. *After another verbal barrage, Andrew left the field, straining so the tears would not gush out. "I'm no good...I'm a failure...I'll never amount to anything, ever."*

What Andrew did not understand was that the negative messages he had heard were lies. Unfortunately, he grew up with a view that equated being yelled at with obedience. How many "Andrews" do you know? One of the most severe warnings ever issued in history was issued by the Lord Jesus to adults who abuse children:

*"But whosoever causes one of these little ones who believes in Me to stumble, it would be better for him if a millstone were hung around his neck, and he were thrown into the sea."* (Mark 9:42 NKJV)

# THE LORD'S DAY

The Lord's Day is not a day of fasting in solitude, but of feasting: eating and drinking in the presence of the Lord, and His people. In this weekly holiday, gathering together with the saints for *lively fellowship, and communion in Christ,* we are made *one* family together by hearing the *same* Word and sharing in *one* Spirit. In this assembly, the kingdom of God is most visibly present in the world in its current form: as an embassy of grace, creating a forgiven and forgiving society. We often hear it taught that nine of the Ten Commandments are interwoven into the New Testament; but often that one commandment left out is not in some cases fully or correctly explained. In giving the Ten Commandments, God based the *fourth (Sabbath)* command on the *imitation* of God by His image-bearer:

*"For in six days the LORD made heaven and earth, the sea, and all that is in them, and rested on the seventh day. Therefore, the LORD blessed the Sabbath day and made it holy."* (Exodus 20:11 ESV)

So, this command is not merely based on Israel's special relationship to God, but on the original relationship of God and humanity in Creation. Therefore, the New Covenant celebration of the Lord's Day is different from its observance under the Old Covenant. We are no longer obligated to the ceremonial laws attached to it in the Mosaic Covenant.

Additionally, the seismic impact of Christ's resurrection moved the Covenant gathering from Saturday to Sunday: the Lord's Day. This day was set aside entirely for the ministry of the communion, Word, teaching, prayer, and fellowship (study prayerfully Acts 2:42; 20:7; 1 Cor. 16:2; Heb. 10:25; Rev. 1:10).

## STUDY GUIDE: CHAPTER 9

1. The initiative in the transformational process of the _____ initially comes from God.

2. This is clear from the biblical imperatives: repent, believe in the _____ _____ in Jesus Christ, and have faith in _____ _____.

3. We must _____ _____ the old person and _____ on the _____ to work out the salvation given to us.

4. The moral teaching of Jesus was His insistence that you cannot keep the law by trying not to break the law.

5. Discipline is by no means all that is involved. In fact they cannot be effective without the Word of the gospel and the Spirit working in tandem in our lives.

6. The Great Commission is a call not only to foreign missions and church planting, but to the succession of covenant blessings from one generation to the next.

7. The seismic impact of Christ's resurrection moved the Covenant celebration from Saturday to Sunday.

# CHAPTER TEN

## What Matters Most

*"Don't copy the behavior and customs of this world, but let God transform you into a new person by changing the way you think. Then you will learn to know God's will for you, which is good and pleasing and perfect."* (Romans 12:2 NLT)

How we react to the challenges and questions of life shows our worldview. This is very critical, making it what matters most. An atheist might stir up a lot of dust against those who believe in God, but at 33,000 feet up in a terrible thunderstorm and turbulence shakes the airplane, a quick prayer may just escape his lips. The Word of God commands that we Christians:

- "Set our minds on things above" (see Colossians 3:2),
- "Be shaped into the image of Christ by the Spirit" (see 2 Corinthians 3:18).

A true Biblical Christian worldview that leads to such transformation matters most. Living out such a worldview is not something we grab ahold of at conversion: it is something that influences how we see and respond to the world in *all* areas of our lives.

Today many of the churches in this country do not disciple their people to follow Christ. Therefore, they neglect the disciplines God uses through the Spirit and the Word working in tandem to sanctify and mature our minds and hearts (souls). So, they favor harmful habits that negatively shape the way they see and engage with others.

Today many of those who strive to follow Christ closely may unknowingly be influenced by a *secular* outlook. As the *secular*

Worldview becomes more distinct and known, true problems develop, however, we begin to see more important and personal issues – such as morality, justice, and fairness – in fundamentally different ways.

Many times two people can have intensely opposite responses to many issues. The same event has the power to provoke widely different reactions from different people, and this is due mainly to a difference in opinions (rational thinking). Take for example, the very different reactions to the Israeli – Hamas war, why are we so surprised by the unexpected negative outcry from our *secularized* institutions of higher learning that produces – our future presidents, judges, senators, and other legislators, professors, corporate executes, and other national and local level leaders?

# WHAT IS A WORLDVIEW?

A worldview is a set of fundamental beliefs that shows the way we see and engage the world. It is through this framework that we interpret everyday life and make decisions. Charles Colson described a worldview as, "the sum total of our beliefs about the world, the "big picture' that directs our daily decisions and actions."[25]

The center of our worldview revolves around how we understand God, ethics, truth, and reality:

- Where did humans come from?
- Does God exist?
- What is truth?
- How do we distinguish between good and evil?
- What is the meaning and purpose of my life?
- Where do we go when we die?

---

[25] Charles Colson, *How Now Shall We Live?* (Carol Stream, IL: Tyndale House, 1999), 14.

Our worldview is comprised of the answers to these and similar questions. Two other important factors to consider:

1. Our physical eyes help us to see, interpret, and interact with the physical world.
2. Our worldview helps us to understand and interact with the moral, social, and spiritual elements of life.

Our worldview is also a product of our decisions, habits, and influences. Certainly, the cultures and communities we live in can have a profound effect on our answers to the fundamental questions above; therefore, many of us have similar worldviews as those people around us. Our worldviews can change over the course of our lives, as we acquire new sources of influence.

***At the same time, a Christian can begin reading the Bible every day – over time, his or her values and beliefs shift as that person learns and applies biblical truths to their life.

---

How we respond to challenges and questions of life *exposes our worldview.*

---

## DEVELOPING A TRUE CHRISTIAN WORLDVIEW

As stated in an earlier section, Scripture calls us to set our minds on things above (see Colossians 3:2) and be shaped into the image of Christ by the Spirit (see 2 Corinthians 3:18). A true Christian worldview that leads to such transformation has certain requirements:

Our Christian worldview is shaped by the influences of the gospel to respond to the world in all areas of our lives. When Christians participate in the ways of the world undoubtedly this transformation has not taken place. They have allowed their worldview to become tainted. It's not hard to find nominal believers in our churches today, especially in those churches where Christians have not been *discipled* to follow Christ. It is so easy for these to be drawn away from the disciplines God uses to sanctify and mature our minds and hearts; and therefore find themselves wrapped up in harmful habits that *negatively* shape the way they see and engage with others.

Today, many people who strive to follow Christ closely may knowingly or unknowingly be swayed by the secular outlook. Sexuality plays a big part in this with many parents. Sympathy and support have swayed many people to deviate from the gospel truth.

Often feeling-oriented rather than true gospel-oriented Christians might give the right answers depicting a Christian worldview and yet when confronted with the major questions of life and identity – he or she may yield. However, if they would take a closer look at their time and thinking, they too, might conclude that their worldview has become disordered.

## CHECK THE SOURCE

As we view the daily activities of college students, there is little doubt that they have been oriented by their secular professors and studies to deconstruct the true Christian worldview for the secular atheistic worldview. Have we parents been silent too long? I heard a comment the other day from a college faculty member concerning who knows what's best for our children, the parents or the educators? If we are not careful both parents and educators will lose out to (money and its (foreign)source of supply with certain ungodly *stipulations*). In essence, they have ignored Paul's exhortation:

> *"Don't copy the behavior and customs of this world, but let God transform you into a new person by changing the way you think. Then you will learn to know God's will for you, which is pleasing and perfect."* (Romans 12:2 NKJV)

## MORE THAN ENOUGH

In a culture afloat in a sea of outrage, and pain, the Christian's worldview frequently does not look very different from those around them who hold secular worldviews. We have the same addictions, play the same political games, reveal the same fears, and anxieties, as our neighbors, and coworkers. When our worldview is markedly similar to that of a person that doesn't know Jesus Christ, what does that say about us? The reality of Christ's:

- Redemptive work
- The indwelling of the Holy Spirit
- Our adoption as coheirs in the kingdom of God

should bring forth a very different worldview. However, Christians too often appear conformed. Instead of appearing changed and renewed. Since you have heard about Jesus and learned the truth that comes from him some Christians feel challenged. We need to hear Paul's exhortation:

> *But that isn't what you learned about Christ. Since you have heard about Jesus and have learned the truth that comes from him, throw off your old sinful nature and your former way of life, which is corrupted by lust and deception. Instead, let the Spirit renew your thoughts and attitudes. Put on your new nature, created to be like God – truly righteous and holy.* (Ephesians 4:20-24 NLT)

While we may be upset or even angry at the level of pure outrage in the world, our first task is putting off the old and putting on the new in ourselves. We must develop the input and output for our lives that will shape our worldviews according to God's truth. What habits have we developed? The answer to this question reveals the truth about our loves and, in turn, what is shaping our worldviews.

Scripture warns us about the quality of voices we allow into our lives. What we see and hear is depicted as the gateway to what we love and worship. The psalmist outlines the way Scripture guides and protects us against sin. Just as important as meditating on God's Word in his exhortation to "turn our eyes away from worthless things" (Psalm 119:37 NIV). Jesus expounds on this in the Sermon on the Mount: "The eye is the lamp of the body. So, if your eye is healthy, your whole body will be full of light, but if your eye is bad, your whole body will be full of darkness. If then the light in you is darkness, how great is the darkness?" (see Matthew 6:22-23).

We should carefully restudy Paul's list in Philippians 4:8 ("whatever is true, whatever is noble, whatever is right, whatever is pure, whatever is lovely, whatever is admirable – if anything is excellent, or praiseworthy," NIV).

## WHATEVER IS TRUE – THINK ON THESE THINGS

Psychologists have long warned us about the peril to personality of an unrelieved sense of guilt, buried deep in the subconscious, working like a cancer in the health of moral life. However, it is also dangerous to let pass easily the occasions when we have used our freedom "for an occasion to the flesh" and not to gain increased freedom from *self* in the larger purposes of our Creator.

The pain of the *spirit* when we make *self* rather than God our chief end is a healthy and not a deathly pain, just as the pain that warns us like a tooth's decay. As children, we remembered that a toothache meant a visit to the dentist, and we came up with ways to avoid the remembrance as long as we could. So in all our shortcomings, we like to get over the memory of them as fast as we can. There is a moment of "feeling sorry," and then we try to leave the "guilty thing" behind and act as if it never happened.

But our past is never left behind. It is always a part of the present, conditioning it both in ourselves and in others whom we have influenced or hurt. Paul could not take back the lives he had murdered in his mad career as a persecutor, and the memory of that fanatical mistake never left him. Again and again he speaks of it in his letters as though he did not want to forget it. For it stood in his mind as a measure of God's mercy and forgiveness that so grave a sinner could be made into an apostle by the grace of God.

---

Passing regrets over our past doings – have little effect.

---

But the persistent regret that comes in a constantly renewed desire to put one's whole life, consequences and all, in the hands of God is what the Bible means by *"godly sorrow,"* so very different from *being sorry for one's foolish self.*

> It is not gaining that guilt should be wholly forgotten ... But it is gained to win an inner intensity of heart through a deeper and deeper inner sorrowing over guilt ... when consequences even become "redemptive" ... this is the older, the strong and the powerful repentance.[26]

Thus the peace of God can transform all sense of guilt into an unsparing sense of responsibility for all misled and misunderstood and frustrated lives.

The conclusion of this whole matter of the strife of life was given to us in the Prince of Peace, who found no peace for Himself on earth. He stood against the full force of malicious evil, so that He was hated by the authorities and the elite, misunderstood by the masses, deserted by His friends, with no apparent help from God, until the waves of calamity submerged Him completely. Only after the deadliest thing has happened did it become plain that there is a *unity* between the Spirit of God and the spirit of man that remains "beyond tragedy," and survives all the accidents of life or death. Praise God!

> *"Therefore let those who suffer according to God's will do right and entrust their souls to a faithful creator."* (1 Peter 4:19)

And my brothers and my sisters, that really is the conclusion of the whole matter.

---

[26] Soren Kierkegaard, *Purity of Heart* (New York: Harper & Bros, 1938), pp. 17-18.

# IS IT TRUE?

Finally, Paul seeks to impress upon his readers that they must have certain right standards of actions, and determine on each occasion how these should be applied:

- **Whatsoever things are true:** Make sure that you are not mistaking some error for truth. Surprisingly, much of the confusion in the world has been caused by well-meaning people who act conscientiously by rules and convictions which are entirely wrong.
- **Whatsoever things are honest:** Much in our codes of honor are artificial or fake, but there are ways and actions which we know by our deepest convictions to be right. To act contrary to them is an offense against God.
- **Whatsoever things are just:** Paul here employs his word for saving righteousness in its normal sense. Every individual can resolve that in their daily occupation and all social relations to at least deal justly.
- **Whatsoever things are pure:** This is an all-encompassing term. Besides actual wrongs there are many habits and actions which degrade a person in their own eyes and in the eyes of others. As he or she keeps their body clean, they must wash away everything that debases their soul.
- **Whatsoever things are lovely:** meaning "worthy of love." There are some ways of acting and types of character which have charisma (spiritual) about them to which we desire that we could act in that manner.
- **Whatsoever things are of good report:** (or well-spoken of) for example – all men have always agreed should be held in honor and cannot be set aside. Paul stresses moral standards by which conduct should be tested, and he summarizes with, "If there be any virtue, and if there be any praise." For the Christian the only judgment which mattered was that of God's Word and His Spirit: **What you have learned and received and heard and seen in me, do. And the God of peace will be with you.**

Paul offers himself as an example, for his effort had been not only to teach Christianity – but to display it in his own walk and life-living. His readers in past, present, and future generations may be sure of this protection when their one aim is to do what is right, and to be steadfast to their Christian faith.

## THE PEACE OF GOD

Again Paul offers himself as an example, for his effort had been not only to teach Christianity, but to display it in his person. Since it was not just another set of rules – but a new life altogether, it could be presented only through a living human being. He carefully defines:

1. How he had imparted the Christian knowledge.
2. He had done so first by instruction in the principles of the faith.
3. Then he handed down the tradition of how Jesus lived and died.
4. Then by counsels he had given to those who sought his guidance.
5. Then by his personal actions.

Therefore, the Philippians had seen for themselves, while he lived among them, how he had followed the Christian teaching in spite of weakness, temptations, and persecution. They must keep his example before them and act as he had done; and ***the God of peace will be with you.*** Here he returns to what he had already said, *that* the great safeguard of the believer is the peace of God. His readers may be sure of this protection when their one aim is to do God's will and standfast in their Christian faith.

## STUDY GUIDE: CHAPTER 10

1. How we react to the challenges and questions of _____ shows our _____.

2. The Word of God commands that we Christians "set our _____ on the _____ above."

3. We are commanded that we be _____ into the _____ of Christ by the _____ _____.

4. In America today many churches do not _____ their people to follow Christ.

5. The center of our _____ revolves around how we understand _____, _____, _____, and reality.

6. Our worldview is also the product of our _____, _____, and _____.

7. Our Christian worldview is shaped by the influences of the gospel to respond to the world in all areas of our lives. When Christians participate in the ways of the world undoubtedly this transformation has not taken place.

8. In a culture such as ours afloat in a sea of outrage and pain – the Christian's _____ looks very different from those who hold on to the _____ worldview.

# CHAPTER ELEVEN

# When God's Command Becomes A Question

*But a man named Ananias, with his wife Sapphira, sold a piece of property, and kept back some of the proceeds for himself, with his wife's full knowledge, and bringing a portion of it, he laid it at the apostles' feet. But Peter said, "Ananias, why has Satan filled your heart to lie to the Holy Spirit and to keep back some of the proceeds of the land? While it was unsold, did it not remain your own? And after it was sold, was it not under your control? Why is it that you have conceived this deed in your heart? You have not lied to men, but to God ..."* (Acts 5:1-11 NASB)

The problem was, Anaias told them he was contributing the entire amount from the sale. He and Sapphira his wife wanted it to look as though they were very generous giving without the sacrifice. Peter said that such actions were attempts to "test the Spirit of the Lord" (v. 9). In his sermon on the passage, the church father John Chrysostom reflected on why God responded so harshly to their deception. He wrote, "The matter was not one to be simply passed over: like a gangrene, it must be cut out, that it might not infect the rest of the body.[27]

Hollow service begets hollow service. When the world praises fake service, it engenders more by providing the benefits of giving without the actual gift. Such giving uncovers what we are really after – praise!

As is commonly known today, we are a society in which everything is permitted, and nothing is forgiven. To break that down, the world constantly preaches that you can do or be anything you

---

[27] John Chrysostom, "Homily 12 on the Acts of the apostles," *Nicene and post-Nicene Fathers, First Series,* vol 11, ed. Philip Schaff, trans. J. Walker, J. Sheppard, and H. Browne (Buffalo, NY: Christian Literature Publishing Co., 1889), http://www.newadvent.org/fathers/210112.htm.

want until it is *offended* at what you are doing or what you are. Then a switch flips:

- Holiness is *replaced* by autonomy
- And justice is *replaced* by angry rage.

In the midst of this situation, mission, and love need to be focused to a posture of *humility* and *service.*

Sadly, humility and service are two qualities that are becoming hard to find even among the community of faith today. Survey after survey has shown a decline in Bible reading in this country; which I believe is the cause of the mess we are in today. There is ample evidence of that concerning the Israel/ Hamas war in the Middle East.

I was astounded at the way "open lies" flow back and forth concerning waning support for Israel and the slanted media reports toward Hamas. It is quite evident that Satan has stepped up his game (his intentions of annihilation of the Jewish people); wiping out God and godly influence wherever found. However, being uninformed by a lack of the truth of God's Word in their hearts and minds. Therefore, today people are missing the truth intentionally. The believer follows God by separating him or herself from the *unclean.* In fact, he or she is to separate from all who do take part in such sins. Beware of the trap of being a co-conspirator with those who rebel against God. (see 1 John 2:15-16)

Hear-say is not enough, we cannot follow Christ and walk closely with Him if we are not tuned in to what He is telling us.

---

When we tune-out God," the only signal left to be heard is the world!

---

The story is told of a former park ranger at Yellowstone National Park who was leading a group of hikers to a fire lookout. The ranger was so caught-up in telling the group about the beautiful flowers animals that he considered the messages on his cellphone distracting, so he switched it off. Nearing the tower, the ranger was met by a wheezing and breathless lookout guard, who asked him why he had not responded to the messages on his phone. A grizzly bear had been stalking the group, and authorities were trying to warn them of the danger.

Anytime we tune out the messages God has sent us, we put at peril not only ourselves, but also those around us. How important it is that we never turn off God's saving communications!

# THE NEED OF THE HOUR

There are many distractions that leave us in a fog. It is vitally important that the believer not lose sight of his or her one great goal: that of knowing God, of knowing Him personally, of growing in the knowledge of Him more and more. The Church of Ephesus had a great testimony of faith and love – this stirred the apostle Paul to write to them. He knew that the Christian life must never become still. A person has to grow or else he or she will slip backward. Therefore Paul urged the Ephesian believers to grow in the knowledge and power of God. In Ephesians 1:3-14, he had just shared the great blessings of God which were theirs when they first came to personally know God. Now He wanted them to grow in these blessings:

1. Knowing God personally
2. Experiencing the power of God

Therefore, he told them that he prayed for them. The fact of the matter is he never ceased to ask God that they might grow in the knowledge and power of God. We can lose our focus if our priorities are not in proper order.

The need of the hour as the clock approaches the final hour is meeting need for the knowledge and power of God. The *Scripture* says,

> *"That the God of our Lord Jesus Christ, the Father of glory, may give unto you the Spirit of wisdom and revelation in the knowledge of him: The eyes of your understanding being enlightened; that ye may know what the hope of his calling is, and what is the riches of the glory of his inheritance in the saints."* (Ephesians 1:17-18 KJV)

This is the God we are to know. As stated, He is the only living and true God, the God and Father of our Lord Jesus Christ, and the

God of glory. Christians must grow more and more in the knowledge of Him; they must have an ever-increasing knowledge of Him.

## THE GOD WE ARE TO KNOW

The God we are to know is clearly known. He is not the god of our minds and thoughts, nor is He the god of our hands – the god we conceive when we picture what God is like.

- The God we are to know is the God of Jesus Christ, that is, the God whom Jesus worshipped when He was on earth as a Man: The God whom Jesus Christ came to reveal to humanity. There is *no* other God – not a true and living God. If we are really to know God, we must come to know the God whom Christ worshipped and revealed.
- The God we are to know is the Father of glory, that is, the only true and living God. He is the Supreme Majesty and Sovereign LORD of the Universe – the One who is the Supreme intelligence and power of the universe and who has created all and rules over all – the One who is omnipotent (all powerful), omnipresent (present everywhere). He is the One who declares that He has "set His glory *above* the heavens." (Psalms 8:1).

There are three essentials if Christian are to grow in the knowledge of God. Paul prayed unceasingly for God to give them to the believer:

1. To grow in the knowledge of God, the believer must have the *spirit of wisdom*. He or she must seek the wisdom of God more than anything else. It is the person who hungers and thirsts after God and His righteousness that is filled. It is not enough to know facts about God; a person must know God personally. He or she must:

    - Know how to experience the facts of God.
    - Must use the facts to develop a personal relationship with God – a growing relationship with God – that is intimate.

- A relationship that grows deeper and deeper.
- It is not an intellectual knowledge of God, but an experiential knowledge of God.

2. To grow in the knowledge of God a believer must have the *spirit of revelation*. The spirit of revelation is the Holy Spirit who reveals God to the believer. This is made clear by the Word of God:

*"But as it is written, Eye hath not seen, nor ear heard, neither have entered into the heart of man, the things which God has prepared for them that love Him. But God hath revealed them unto us by His Spirit for the Spirit searcheth all things, yea, the deep things of God. For what man knoweth the things of a man, save the spirit of man which is in him? Even so the things of God knoweth no man, but the Spirit of God. Now we have received, not the spirit of the world, but the spirit which is of God; that we might know the things that are freely given to us of God."* (1 Corinthians 2:9-12 KJV)

The New Covenant believer is indwelt by the Spirit of God (see John 14:16-17; 14-26; 16:12-15; 1 Corinthians 6:19-20; 2 Corinthians 6:16). The Spirit of God dwells in him or her to teach them the deeper things of God. But notice what the believer must do to grow in the knowledge of God [the spirit of revelation] ... a spirit that drives after God; a spirit that seeks to know God, and a spirit that hungers and thirsts after God above all else. The word "revelation" means to manifest, to reveal; to unveil; to uncover; to open. It is the work of the Holy Spirit to reveal the knowledge of God to Christians.

In fact it is the work of the Holy Spirit to reveal the meaning of all truth to the Christian (see John 14:26; 16:12-15). This is further amplified in 1 Corinthians 1:9-16. Here the wisdom of the world is contrasted with the wisdom of God. A spiritual Christian sees (through the Spirit revealing to him or her) the meaning behind world events of history and human experience. Therefore, the Christian gains a growing knowledge day by day. Again, the Christian must seek to have the truth of God revealed to him or her.

3. To grow in the knowledge of God, the rich and deeper things of God, a Christian must have the *eyes of his or her heart enlightened*. The heart must be opened so that the light of God can be seen and grasped. An open heart is the responsibility of both the Christian and the Holy Spirit. The Christian must open his or her heart and focus its love, intelligence, and will upon knowing God. The Christian must seek the Holy Spirit to enlighten and flood his or her heart with the things of God.

*"For God, who commanded the light to shine out of darkness, hath shined in our hearts, to give the light of the knowledge of the glory of God in the face of Jesus Christ."* (2 Corinthians 4:6 KJV)

We must exude God's light. We have to reflect it and radiate it. In Ephesians 5:8-10, we are admonished to: "Walk as children of light (for the fruit of the Spirit is in all goodness, righteousness, and truth), finding out what is acceptable to the Lord." I mourn about the way this *present darkness* is casting its shadows over many Christians and churches.

Sadly, too many people of faith are attempting to blend the light and darkness, thinking they are achieving an acceptable grayness. This doesn't work, and it shows and dims the community of faith's light through trying to overrule God's Word as we increasingly prioritize self, money, and pleasure over God and the things of God.

As we strive to navigate our way through this unfriendly world of end time people that the Bible describe as – "Evil men and imposters will grow worse and worse, deceiving and being deceived." As you feel this increasing pressure to let go of your faith, decide instead to stay in the race and never give up! Remember Jesus is with you. He will keep you from falling. It is His intention to present you faultless before the Father once your race comes to an end.

## THE RESULTS OF KNOWING GOD

God has called us to *stand* before Him in the name and righteousness of Jesus Christ. To stand before Him just as Jesus Christ stands before Him – perfect. It is evident that we are not perfect, not yet anyway. But the day is coming when we shall be. Right now we experience the blessings of God only in part. But when the glorious Day of Redemption comes. We shall be made just like Him. Righteous, and perfect, enabled to live in God's presence, worshipping and serving forever. This is the believer's hope; this is the believer's calling. Jesus modeled this for us when He washed His disciples' feet without exception and expectation: (see John 13:1-17).

This was not a simple demonstration, but an example of perfect service that reflected Jesus' humility while He was here on the earth. Jesus then asked His disciples to imitate Him in washing one another's feet. Jesus wants *us* to serve others humbly and lovingly in every human gesture. As we see Jesus more clearly, the gospel gets bigger and bigger in our hearts:

- His death and resurrection is more astonishing.
- Sin becomes more disgusting.
- The devil and end time people (of the world) seem more evil.

As a result, the restoring work of the Holy Spirit gets mightier. The global extent of the gospel becomes more important. The world is growing eviler, can it be because we have become more selfish? Many churches returned to business as usual after COVID-19. They have picked up their old church program and schedule; which is just that "a program." However, many of us have realized the great frustration and effort the world is going through trying to find the truth of God! As we went visual with our services people across the globe and around the corner contacted us – wanting more of the *truth* of God's Word.

## WHAT ARE WE MAKING (PRODUCING)?

Churches are reminded that "making disciples" continues to be the *command* of Christ – no question about it! Although much of the American church has asked the question (?). Some churches are buying into Satan's deception, claiming the church to be antiqued, old-fashioned, and not relevant. But, through all of the storms the Church and Christians have had to weather over the past two thousand years – Christ has not posted any changes to His Word of command ("make disciples!"). We are still here for that purpose – remember, it takes a disciple to make a disciple. As I pointed out in an earlier section, much of the church has turned to rationalization, setting aside the guidance of the Word of God and the Spirit of God and have bit into Satan's cultural Christianity secular intellectual model. Some people are turning to a god their mind has produced for them. Others are seeking a spiritual experience, but through the spirit of this world, based on their emotions (feelings). In a sense many are simply adding to the already mental problem many experts claim America is experiencing today. There is a solution to our problem, but it requires a turning back to the true and living God. Read on.

## UNITY THROUGH HUMILITY

In the true church of Jesus Christ, the rich and poor gather on the same footing, without distinction, in Christ between Jews and Gentiles, men and women, no matter the race or color (see 1 Corinthians 12:3; Galatians 3:28; Colossians 3:11; James 2:1-6). People were also divided in Paul's day over various issues. Topics like what foods were permissible to eat and what days were considered holy brought disagreement among the Christians in Rome. Despite being "fully convinced in their own mind" on which position they held; Paul reminds them of their *common ground*: living for Jesus! (see Romans 14:5-9) Instead of passing judgment on one another, he encouraged them to "do what leads to peace and to mutual edification."(v. 19)

Also we find this truth weaved into Paul's message to the Ephesian church a powerful implication:

- Despite the differences between the early Christians – there is an underlying unity.
- Please understand, this unity is not produced by believers.
- No where does the apostle tell the church to strive to produce unity.
- Instead he admonishes them to *maintain the unity that is already there.*

This unity can only be produced by the Holy Spirit. However, once produced, the believers are responsible to maintain it through Christlike love "for one another." As was seen in an earlier section, Jesus *commanded* us to "love one another." Unity is a godly and spiritual characteristic. Again, through rationalization, most churches are willing to settle for autonomous manmade union, a semblance of true unity. Again, we have a case of man questioning (?) the command of God to the point settling for a cultural entity. That is why Paul puts forth such a great effort to make sure there is no *misunderstanding* of the true nature of the unity of the Spirit he wrote,

*"There is one body, and one Spirit, just as you were called in one hope of your calling, one Lord, one faith, one baptism, one God and Father of all, who is above all, and through all, and in you all."* (Ephesians 4:4-6 NKJV)

Herein is the true unity of the Body of Christ, we see God's answer to Jesus' prayer in Gethsemane: **"That they may be one; even as thou, Father, art in me, and I in thee,"** (John 17:21 KJV). Emphasis added. As I stated in my book, *"Out of Babylon,"* [28]It is true that a body is an organization, but the body is so much more. The body of Christ consists of thousands of cells with *one mutually shared life* – bound together as an organism in bodily unity. Here is the mystery or secret of the body – all parts share *one life* together!

---

Here is the mystery or secret of the body – all parts share *one life together.*

---

The purpose for walking worthy is *onefold – unity.* Believers are to work at keeping the peace so that they can remain bonded together in the unity of God's Spirit. Jesus Christ has broken down all walls and barriers existing between people. Every person is precious in the sight of God. When a person approaches God through Jesus Christ, he or she comes like everyone else:

---

[28] Jay Leach, *Out of Babylon: We are not Ignorant of Satan's Devices"* (Trafford Publishing 2023) 105

- On the same grounds and on the same level. He or she is no better or no worse than anybody else, who stands in need of God's forgiveness; along with everyone else.
- They are bowing before Christ and accepting Him as their Lord and Master. Wealth, position, and social status are all forgotten. The only thing that matters is "the salvation and life which Christ offers."
- The point is: when a person comes to Christ in such a spirit, the Spirit of God enters their life and binds the person to all other believers. All divisiveness, differences, and prejudices are set aside; and a spirit of love, peace, and unity exists. So true!

Within the church there is a *prevailing spirit of peace* wrought by God's Spirit. However, there is a tragic fact: not every believer walks in the Spirit – not all the time. Too often, believers miss God's best as they allow *self* and the *old life* through giving in to:

- Prejudices
- Differences
- Hurts
- Jealousies
- Complaints
- Criticisms
- Grumblings
- Gripes
- Pride
- Arrogance
- Comparisons
- Dislikes

The result is catastrophic for the church: divisiveness and disturbance of the peace and spirit of unity. This is the reason for this change. The word used "endeavor." It means being diligent, working to take care, doing one's very best.

God will sometimes allow us to go through challenges and hardships so that we can be molded into what He's called us to be. He waits in anticipation for us to come out of the trials of life "mature and complete not lacking anything" (James 1:4). By staying grounded in

Jesus, we can persevere through any challenge, growing stronger and ultimately allowing the *fruit of the Spirit* to blossom in our lives (see Galatians 5:22-23).

The only way to walk worthy of God's great calling individually and corporately is to work at keeping the peace and unity which God has given us. Nothing cuts the heart of God like divisiveness between His people, divisiveness which tears apart His church.

The very thing God is doing is creating a *new* body of people to live together in the love and unity of His Son. He is going to create a new heaven and earth in which there will be no other spirit. Therefore, He expects us to live in the love and unity of His Spirit now.

*"Now I beseech you, brethren, by the name of our Lord Jesus Christ, that ye all speak the same thing, and that there be no divisions among you; but that ye be perfectly joined together in the same mind and in the same judgment."* (1 Corinthians 1:10 KJV)

As my wife and I have traveled the globe together in the military, and ministry, we have truly experienced the basic unity of the Spirit which already exists among true Christians in the body of Christ. No matter the theological, political, geographical, cultural, or racial differences between us and other believers the mutual life in Christ is immediately evident.

Praise God! Even in these trying times – there remains a sense of belonging to each other. The shared love and Spirit of God within us will not allow any thoughts or things that might try to interrupt or break the unity of the Spirit. Praise the Lord!

## ILLUSTRATION

Simply put, division is a wall between two sides: I was stationed in West Germany during the early 60's when the Berlin Wall was being constructed by the Communists of East Germany to prevent East Germans from uniting with West Germans. That prevention was made clear by the many signs and other indicators that it meant sure death to try to scale the wall. Many people were killed trying to scale the wall that divided the East from the West.

This wall of division separated friends from friends and family from family. The result of this division brought death and despair. At times, it seemed that the wall would stay up forever.

**But God** had another plan. The Communist world was turned upside down as the people in Communist countries were swept up in a global wave of nationalism and the desire for freedom. The Berlin Wall had no power against the forces of unity and freedom – and the Wall came down – and became prize souvenirs for collectors.

Today churches without the presence and operation of the Holy Spirit within and between believers are on life support at best. In some churches various types of the Berlin Wall are being constructed. The only way to keep unity and peace in the church between believers is to remain in the Spirit. In Ephesians 5:18 we are *commanded* to "be filled with the Spirit" (a continuous action). All the glory belongs to God!

# STUDY GUIDE – CHAPTER 11

1. The incident of Ananias and his wife Sapphira was they said they gave a certain amount of money (saying they gave all, but they only presented a portion). In his rebuke to them, Peter said, "such actions were attempts to "_____" the _____ of _____."

2. Hollow service begets _____ _____.

3. We are a society in which everything is _____, and nothing is _____.

4. The believer follows God by separating him or herself from the _____.

5. The need of the hour is meeting needs for the _____ and _____ of God.

6. To grow in the knowledge of God, the believer must have the _____ of _____ more than anything else.

7. To grow in the knowledge of God, a believer must have the Spirit of _____.

# CHAPTER TWELVE

# Apostasy Rising

*"Now, brethren, concerning the coming of our Lord Jesus Christ and our gathering together to Him, we ask you, not to be soon shaken in mind or troubled, either by spirit or by word or by letter, as if from us, as though the day of Christ had come. Let no one deceive you by any means; for that Day will not come unless the falling away comes first, and the man of sin is revealed, the son of perdition."* (2 Thessalonians 2:1-3; also see 2 Timothy 3)

The number of Christians falling away from Christ and His gospel is heartbreaking and yet prophetic. This falling away is not new. Throughout history, many have taken up the banner of Christ only to put down again. Even the first generation of Christians faced this dilemma. When the apostle Paul wrote to the Colossians and to Philemon, he sent them greetings from his coworker Demas who was at his side (see Col. 414; Philem. 1:24). But notice in his final letter, Paul told Timothy, "Demas has forsaken me, having loved this present world." (2 Tim. 4:10)

Sixty years ago when many pastors spoke of the great falling away, some spoke in conjunction with empty pews in the sanctuary on Sunday morning and the popularity of the television set. Overtime churches lost the (public) community to sports, leisure and other activities. Today we find that definition somewhat lacking due to rapid changes in the world and not for the better. As individuals, families, and societies we are experiencing a breakdown that seems impossible to reverse.

Jesus' half-brother, Jude, the son of Joseph and Mary, devoted his short epistle to this very topic. Jude stated his purpose for writing, "To contend earnestly for the faith which was once for all delivered to the saints" (v. 3). Certainly, it helps to realize the apostles faced the same problem of "falling away" that we are witnessing today.

Additionally, we are seeing an acceleration of apostasy in our times. Like Demas many professing Christians find the world more attractive, and they just walk away; while others search for a bloodless religion which require no action or responsibility on their part. Some people that I have spoken with in this condition claim that they still are connected to Christ. The choice is theirs. Earlier I spoke of the value of daily Bible reading and meditation (please review that section in Chapter 10). "Where the Spirit of the Lord is there is liberty."(see 2 Corinthians 3:17)

Although evil has always been a part of human society, including extreme brutality and violence; Satan and his demons have been countered by the Spirit and the Word in the saints. But today as the Spirit and the Word are hindered and *rejected* by a lack of knowledge of the truth among believers, Satan's activities have been increasing dramatically. Gun violence, homicides, addictions, depression, and the list goes on. Why is this happening? In this country (US) and the West survey after survey attributes this to the lack of Bible Reading/ study resulting in people letting go of *the faith*. Personally, I agree. The Bible influenced and profoundly affected all the above-mentioned sin (s) and much more. A watered-down gospel assists the evil one in all of his strategies in the absence of the Bible's counterpunch (the true gospel of Christ, 1 Corinthians 15:1-4). A broken gospel is ineffective for treating and healing broken people. Something is significantly broken in humanity. In Paul's last letter he predicted nineteen specific characteristics of how end time people will behave during the last days before the Tribulation:

"But know this, he wrote, "that in the last days perilous times will come. For end-time people will be:

1. Lovers of themselves
2. Lovers of money
3. Boasters
4. Proud
5. Blasphemers
6. Disobedient to parents
7. Unthankful

8. Unholy
9. Unloving
10. Unforgiving
11. Slanderers
12. Without self-control
13. Brutal
14. Despisers of good
15. Traitors
16. Headstrong
17. Haughty
18. Lovers of pleasure rather than lovers of God
19. Having a form of godliness but denying its power" [29]

Then he added: "But evil men and imposters will grow worse and worse, deceiving and being deceived."[30] Paul prophesied, people will spiral downward in accelerated godlessness and more darkness as we approach the Tribulation. As followers of Christ, we are no longer in the kingdom of darkness, but now we are children of light. Today it is imperative that we walk and live as children of light.

The Psalmist says, "They looked to Him and were radiant, and their faces were not ashamed." (Psalm 34:5). Isaiah says, "Then you shall see and become radiant, and your heart shall swell with joy." (Isaiah 60:5)

## SHINE, SHINE, SHINE

The Scripture exhorts every child of God, "… You were once darkness, but now you are light in the Lord. Walk as children of light." (Ephesians 5:8) Therefore, God sees believers as having already been raised and exalted to live eternally with Him – all because He sees them in Christ Jesus. He sees their faith and counts them as being *in Christ Jesus.*

---

[29] 2 Timothy 3:1-5)
[30] 2 Timothy 3:13)

*"But if the Spirit of him that raised up Jesus from the dead dwell in you, he that raised up Christ from the dead shall also quicken your mortal bodies by his Spirit that dwelleth in you."* (Romans 8:11)

In order to enjoy the great promises of God, we have to be *in Christ.*[31] This is the wonderful truth of this verse and point. God by His mercy has made us sit in heavenly places *in Christ Jesus.* The work of God's mercy has one great purpose – to show believers the riches of His grace throughout all the ages to come. God has done so much for us through Christ Jesus that it will take an eternity to show it all off.

I heard an illustration about a backslidden preacher who bowed before God and all of a sudden, a vision popped up before his eyes. He saw himself in the manner of a dog slinking up to his owner after a mischievous act. Knowing that the owner was going to seriously punish him. The idea here is many of us come after sinning and forgiven, slinking up to the throne of grace (in fear) that God is mad with us. We should come "boldly" to the throne of grace, knowing that Christ died on the cross, His blood for all sins. Have you really accepted that fact? It seems to some too good to be true. It is true (praise God)! Again, "Come boldly to the throne of grace that you might receive help in time of need." (Hebrews 4:16) If Satan can keep us slinking-back what kind of witness does that make us?

*"Then shall the righteous shine forth as the sun in the kingdom of their Father. Who hath ears to hear, let him hear."* (Matthew 13:43 KJV)

---

[31] Accessed 11/19/23 https:lifeway.com. To be in Christ means to have a spiritual union with Jesus as a result of one's salvation. It means that believers are identified with Jesus' death, burial, resurrection, and ascension, and share in His life and glory. It also means to have a personal relationship with Christ that is the distinctive mark of His authentic followers. Being in Christ is the basis for our forgiveness, sanctification, and eternal life.

# LET'S CHANGE GEARS

We'll take a look at two trophy cases and what it takes to be a proud owner of one of the trophies.

*A loser again. Satan thought for sure this time that he would add Martin to his trophy collection. He had his game plan outlined in sinister detail: blind him from seeing the gospel during his formative youthful years, offer him the lie that he could take care of his own problems, hook him with addictions, and destroy his marriage. "By the time I'm through with him, he will be all mine," Satan thought to himself. So confident was he, that he began his celebration early by giving a thumbs-up to his demon henchmen. "Boys, take some time. Martin is going in our trophy case."*

*Martin lived most of his adult life in the gutter. Over the years, his heart had become so hard as a rock. He would scoff with disdain wherever anyone would share the gospel with him.*

*"I don't need any religion. I'm a man's man," was his rehearsed speech. Over the course of life, he became an alcoholic which ruined his career and marriage. By the time he was 50 years old, he was as good as dead, an accident waiting to happen.*

*Unknown to Martin, God was at work in his life. Martin did not know that God also has a trophy case that is filled with trophies that resembled Martin. God takes personal pleasure in redeeming people just like Martin and in showing them off as trophies of His mercy.*

*Thus God had a plan for Martin's life: replace his heart of stone with a heart of flesh, open his eyes to see his need for a Savior, and allow other believers to have a burden for him. God to heal Martin from his addictions and provide a new Christian wife who would be a helpmate to him.*

*The result: Martin became a trophy of God's mercy. He was saved. He was added to God's great trophy case of believers, of people who have experienced God's great mercy. Now, whose trophy, are you?*

# STUDY GUIDE: CHAPTER 12

What is happening in our churches today is heartbreaking and discouraging as Christians are following away from Christ and His gospel – that is to have taken up the banner of Christ only to put it down and walk away *from Him.*

1. Several decades ago the emphasis was the backsliders and empty pews, but today it's _____.

2. As individuals, families, and societies we are _____ a breakdown that seems impossible to reverse. What happened?

3. Something is significantly _____ in humanity. Crimes and mayhem have _____ increased.

4. The apostle Paul predicted nineteen specific characteristics of how people will _____ during the last days before the Tribulation (Prayerfully study 2 Timothy 3:1-5).

5. The Scripture exhorts every child of God, "you were once in _____ but now you are _____ in the Lord."

6. In order to enjoy the great promises of God, we must be _____ _____.

7. Therefore, God sees believers as having already been raised and exalted to live eternally with Him – because He sees them _____ _____.

# SECTION FOUR

# THE QUESTION IS

# CHAPTER THIRTEEN

# Mercy — Oh! What A Relief It Is!

*"And you were dead in your trespasses and sins, in which you formerly walked according to the course of this world, according to the prince of power of the air, of the spirit that is now working in the sons of disobedience. Among them we too all formerly lived in the lusts of our flesh, indulging the desires of the flesh and of the mind, and were by nature children of wrath, even as the rest.*

*But God, being rich in mercy, because of His great love with which He loved us, even when we were dead in our transgressions, made us alive together with Christ (by grace you have been saved), and raised us up with Him, and seated us with Him in the heavenly places, in Christ Jesus, in order that in the ages to come He might show the surpassing riches of His grace in kindness toward us in Christ Jesus.* (Ephesians 2:1-7 NASB)

"But God," the apostle Paul writes, "being rich in mercy." Notice the sequence, it begins with God's love connecting Him with a sinful person, which activates His grace, in turn, putting in motion His mercy.[32] God loves us not because of something within us, but something within Himself. And in His love, He demonstrates His grace, which brings forgiveness. Then grace prompts mercy and praise God, there is the needed relief!'

The wonder of mercy is that it is demonstrated to the offender as well as to the victim. When the offender realizes his or her

---

[32] Mercy means *relief, price paid, even for the 8uoffender also.* Webster's New Explorer Dictionary and Thesaurus. (Federal Street Press, Springfield, MA 1999) 324

wrong – God brings mercy. When the victim needs help to go on – God gives mercy.

---

## THE WORK OF GOD'S MERCY HAS ONE GREAT PURPOSE – TO SHOW BELIEVERS THE RICHES OF HIS GRACE THROUGHOUT ALL THE AGES TO COME. PRAISE HIM!

---

## OUR SOURCE OF RELIEF – MERCY

God, our compassionate and loving heavenly Father, is the author of relief.

At times when doing His will, it results in the unexpected – but His mercy comes to make it bearable.

The Bible says of us,

> *"And you were dead in your trespasses and sins, in which you formerly walked according to the course of this world, according to the prince of the power of the air, of the spirit that is now working in the sons of disobedience. Among them we too all formerly lived in the lusts of our flesh, indulging the desires of the flesh and of the mind, and were by nature children of wrath, even like the rest.*
>
> *But God, being rich in mercy, because of His great love with which He loved us, even when we were dead in our transgressions, made us alive together with Christ (by grace you have been saved), and raised up with Him, and seated us with Him in the heavenly places, in Christ Jesus, in order that in the ages to come He might show the surpassing riches of His grace n kindness toward us in Christ Jesus."* (Ephesians 2:1-7 NASB)

"But God," the apostle Paul writes, "being rich in mercy." As already stated in this section: The connecting link between a holy God and a sinful person is God's love, which activates His grace, which in turn, sets His mercy in motion. And in His love He demonstrates His grace – which brings forgiveness. And not only that, but grace moves mercy – resulting in relief. Certainly we should be encouraged and strengthened by Paul's personal testimony, he writes,

> *"I thank Christ Jesus our Lord, who has strengthened me, because He considered me faithful, putting me into service; even though I was formerly a blasphemer and a persecutor and a violent aggressor. And yes, I was shown mercy, because I acted ignorantly in unbelief.* (1 Timothy 1:12-13 NASB)

In this passage of Scripture, Paul gives three descriptions of his former life:

1. "I was a *blasphemer.*" The word means "an insulter." I insulted God's people.
   I was angry at Christians. I accused them of crimes against God.
2. "I was a *persecutor.*" He took every means under Jewish law to hurt, to humiliate, even annihilate, Christians.
3. And then, I was a violent *aggressor.*" The Greek word suggests a kind of *"arrogant sadism."* It describes a person who is out to inflict pain and injury for the sheer joy of inflicting it. "*I* loved to make them squirm. I loved to make them cry. I loved to see them removed from this earth.[33]

Certainly this is not usually thought of Paul in this manner, but that's the way he describes himself before Christ. God showed him mercy – and He does the same for us. (O What a relief it us).

---

[33] Charles R. Swindoll, *The Mystery of God's Will,* (Word Publishing, NASHVILLE) 121

## STUDY GUIDE: CHAPTER 13

1. "… Even when we were dead in our transgressions, God made us alive together with _____."

2. The wonder of mercy is that it is demonstrated to the _____ as well as to the _____.

3. When the offender realizes his or her _____ God brings mercy.

4. The connecting link between a holy God and a sinful person is God's love, which activates His grace, which in turn sets His mercy in motion.

5. Additionally, grace moves _____ resulting in relief.

6. In 1 Timothy 1:12-13, Paul gives three descriptions of his former life:

   _____, _____, _____.

7. Certainly this is not usually the way we think of Paul, but God should God showed him mercy – and He does the same focus.

# CHAPTER FOURTEEN

# The World's Right To Judge Believers

⊷┼ ╪◈╪ ┼⊶

*"A new commandment I give to you, that you love one*
*another. By this all will know that you are My disciples. If*
*you have love for one another." (John 13:34-35 NKJV)*

As followers of Christ, we must always be mindful that His gospel isn't something we simply believe – but something we do. Something we must practice by *choosing* to love other people. Jesus said, "A new commandment I give to you, that you love one another, as I have loved you, that you also love one another. By this all will know that you are My disciples, if you have love for another" (John 13:34-35).

In his book, *The Mark of a Christian,* the late Francis Schaffer pointed out that Jesus gave the world the right to judge believers by their love for one another. Upon His authority Jesus gave the world the right to judge whether you and I are truly born-again Christians on the basis of our observable love toward all Christians.[34]

---

Jesus said, "A new commandment I give to you, that you love one another. By this *all will know* that you are My disciples – if you have love for one another." (John 13:34-35 NKJV) Emphasis mine.

---

First John 4 reveals to us that when we live in truth and love, speaking it with our words and intentions – God reveals more of Himself to us, perfecting [maturing] His love in us. He does this so

---

[34] Francis A. Schaeffer, *The Mark of the Christian* (Downers Grove, Il. InterVarsity Press, 1970), 22-23.

that as we abide in Him more and more, we then reveal more of His love to others. Notice:

- "Beloved, let us love one another, for love is of God and everyone who loves is born of God and knows God" (v. 7).
- "No one has seen God at any time; if we love one another, God abides in us, and His love is perfected in us" (v. 12).
- "By this we know that we abide in Him and He in us, because He has given us His Spirit" (v. 13).
- "We have come to know and have believed the love which God has for us. God is love, and the one who abides in love abides in Him" (v. 16).
- "There is no fear in love; but perfect love casts out fear, because fear involves punishment, and the one who fears is not perfected in love" (v. 18).
- "And this commandment we have from Him, that the one who loves God should love His brother also" (v. 21). NASB

## LOVING AS CHRIST LOVED

Before a person can follow Christ, he or she must commit and attach themselves to Christ. That means surrendering their life to Him and then begin to follow Him. The word "followers" means imitators. Some prefer the translation, that we are to become imitators of God. Just as children learn by imitating their parents, so are we to learn by imitating God. The very idea that we are to be followers and imitators of God is a bold idea. Just imagine, Scripture boldly proclaims that we are to become like God!

- Christ said, *"Be ye therefore perfect, even as your Father which is in heaven is perfect."* (Matthew 5:48 KJV)
- God demanded: *"Ye shall be holy: for I the LORD your God am holy."* (Leviticus 19:2 KJV)
- Paul declared: *"But we all ... are changed into the same image [of Christ] from glory to glory."* (2 Corinthians 4:18 KJV)

- Peter charged: *"But as He which hath called you is holy, so be ye holy in all manner of conversation; because it is written, Be ye holy; for I am holy."* (1 Peter 1:15-16 KJV)

Therefore, the believer follows God, by loving as Christ loved. We must pray for God to help us to learn more and more of His love – and we must make the request often every day.

*"But God commended His love toward us, in that, while we were yet sinners, Christ died for us. Much more then, being now justified by His blood, we shall be saved from wrath through Him. For if, when we were enemies, we were reconciled to God by the death of His Son, much more, being reconciled to God, we shall be saved by His life."* (Romans 5:8-10 KJV) This is *agape love;* the very same love God has for us.

## THE CHRISTIAN BELIEVER'S WALK

While I've never met a person who took a test without wanting to know what to study before. Try to imagine a pilot who wants his or her airplane to lose power at 33000 feet up in the air. What about a soldier who is willing to go into battle without his weapon? I've never met any such person, have you?

But I have met Christians who were perfectly willing to live their lives without the *power of the Holy Spirit.* Why is this so true today? Many possibly are ignorant of His power. Others know about the power of the Holy Spirit but would rather live in their own strength and power.

If we Christians deny the love of God and the Holy Spirit, who was promised and sent by Christ Himself to (help us) lead and guide us (prayerfully study John 14, 16, Acts 1:8); the results spill out into how we live our lives. We take our relationship with God and turn it into just another religion without the Holy Spirit. Without the power of God, Christianity becomes an empty form (Cultural Christianity). Or as Paul told Timothy, "Having a form of godliness, but denying the power of God." (2 Timothy 3:5 NKJV) Only by His strength and direction are we able to succeed.

Have you surrendered to the Holy Spirit's power and control by acknowledging your weakness and recognizing His power, omniscience, and wisdom?

Jesus Christ Himself is our peace. Christ brings us peace when we realize that He died for us, offering us deliverance from the bondage of sin and death and a life of eternity with God. He also brings a deeper sense of peace when we realize that He gives us the daily power to overcome the aggravating and terrible weight of anguish, guilt, loneliness, empties, and fear.

Christ brings a still deeper sense of peace when we realize that He has brought perfect love and unity to the world – that He has eliminated all divisions and barriers and differences between God and man and between men. All men now approach God on the same basis, on an equal footing: by the blood of Jesus Christ. There is no other way.

Therefore, when a person comes to the cross, he or she comes with everyone else who is standing at the feet of Jesus. He stands as one with them – all on an equal basis: sinners who need a Savior. No one standing there, is accepted by God because he or she is better, healthier, wealthier, more intelligent, more capable, or more religious than anyone else.

One is acceptable to God because he or she acknowledges their unworthiness and nothingness and desperate need – to be saved by the blood of Jesus Christ. Thus, they are acceptable to God because he or she is as all other men – lost and needful – and comes as one with all other people to confess Christ as their Savior.

---

**"Peace I leave with you, My peace I give unto you: not as the world giveth, give I unto you. Let not your heart be troubled, neither let it be afraid." (John 14:27 KJV)**

---

All who come to Christ for salvation receive a common love and purpose and work.

1. There is common love. Every believer who comes to Jesus Christ loves Him, and that common love among believers stirs love for all those whom Christ loves – which is everyone.
2. There is the common purpose and work: that of living righteously and bearing testimony to the glorious message of salvation and to life eternal.

---

**"But if we walk in the light, as he is in the light, we have fellowship one with another, and the blood of Jesus Christ his Son cleanseth from all sin."** (1 John 1:7 KJV)

---

# YOU ARE GOD'S WORKMANSHIP

You are God's workmanship created in Christ Jesus. The believer experiences two creations – both a natural birth and a spiritual birth. The spiritual birth is the point of this verse. When a person believes in Jesus Christ, God creates that person in Christ. What does that mean?

It **means** that God *[quickens the spirit]* of the believer making his or her spirit alive. Whereas the believer's spirit was dead to God, God creates it anew and makes it alive to God.

---

*"And you hath He quickened, who were dead in trespasses and sins."* (Eph. 2:1 KJV) *"Even when we were dead in sins, [God] hath quickened us together with Christ, (by grace ye are saved)."* (Ephesian 2:5 KJV) Emphasis mine throughout.

---

It **means** that God causes the believer to be *born again spiritually*.

---

*"Jesus answered and said unto him, Verily, verily, I say unto thee, except a man be born again, of water and of the Spirit, he cannot enter into the kingdom of God. That which is born of the flesh is flesh; and that which is born of the Spirit is spirit."* (John 3:3, 5:6 KJV)

---

It **means** that God actually places His *divine nature* into the heart of the believer.

---

*"Whereby are given unto us exceeding great and precious promises: that by these ye might be partakers of the divine nature, having escaped the corruption that is in the world through lust."* (2 Peter 1:4 KJV)

---

It **means** that God actually makes a *new creature* of the believer.

---

*"Therefore if any man be in Christ, he is a new creature: old things are passed away; behold, all things are become new."* (2 Corinthians 5:17 KJV)

---

It **means** that God actually creates a *new man,* which after God is created in Christ.

---

*"And that ye put on the new man which after God is created in righteousness and true holiness."* (Ephesians 4:24 KJV)

---

It **means** that God *renews the believer* by the Holy Spirit.

---

*"Not by works of righteousness which we have done, but according to his mercy he saved us, by the washing of regeneration, and <u>renewing of the Holy Ghost</u>."* (Titus 3:5 KJV)

---

## WE ARE CREATED TO DO GOOD WORKS

God saves a person *for* good works not *by* good works. The believer does not create the beauty, the art that shows in the canvas of his or her life. The believer just shows that he or she is God's workmanship by the life they display. Works are evidence of salvation. Those who walk in trespasses and sins show that they are not God's workmanship – no matter what profession they make (see Ephesians 2:1-2). God's people give ample evidence of the *power of a new life* which operates within them.

Note that God has *ordained* us to walk in good works. Doing good works is not an option for the Christian believer; it is the very nature of the believer. If a person has been created in Christ – if God has worked in him – that person does good works. Their very nature dictates it. Though he or she is not perfect, and they fail; they will keep coming back to God and falling upon their knees, believing and asking forgiveness, and getting back up and going forth once again to do all they can do.

As stated, it is the believer's changed nature – a new creature created to do good works. Therefore, he or she who does them, are like a tree – bears the fruit of their nature. Candlelight services is a favorite tradition because of the wonder of the flickering light as it pierces the darkness. It's a beautiful reminder that the baby Jesus we celebrate on Christmas came *"as a light to shine in this dark world"* (see John 12:46).

Here Christ Himself declared that His purpose in coming to earth was so that all who put their trust in [Him] will no longer remain in the dark. Like the feeling of sitting in a dark sanctuary, there is a vivid reality of living in darkness:

- The discouragement and pain of suffering
- The disorienting feeling of our own helplessness

Jesus came as a human because He didn't want anyone to have to stay in that darkness. Instead, He offers us *light,* in the form of a relationship with Him [in Him], so that we can know peace and joy. And once we have His light living in us, we can shine as lights to a hurting world:

> *"Ye are the light of the world. A city that is set on a hill cannot be hid."* (v. 14)
> *"Let your light so shine before men, that they may see your good works and glorify your Father which is in heaven."* (Matthew 5:16 KJV)

# STUDY GUIDE: CHAPTER 14

1. Jesus said, I give you a new commandment that you love one another. By this _____ _____ _____ that you are My disciples.
2. Beloved, let us love one another, for love is of God and everyone who loves God is _____ of God and _____ God.
3. Before a person can follow Christ, he or she must commit and attach themselves to Christ.
4. God demanded: "Ye shall be holy: for I the LORD your God am holy."
5. Just as children learn by imitating their parents, so are we to learn by imitating God.
6. God saves a person for good works not by good works.
7. Not by works of righteousness which we have done, but according to His *mercy* He saved us, by the washing of regeneration, and renewing of the Holy Ghost (see Titus 3:5).

# CHAPTER FIFTEEN

# *To Live Like Jesus*

An old gospel song prays:

*To be like Jesus, to be like Jesus*
*Oh how I want to be like Him.*
*So meek and lowly*
*So high and holy*
*Oh how I want to be like Him*

In this very hour nowhere is it more needful for His children to live out the compassion of Christ to our world. As the apostle Paul wrote to the church at Colosse:

*So, as those who have been chosen*
*of God,*
*holy and beloved,*
*put on a heart of compassion,*
*kindness, humility, gentleness,*
*and patience.* (Colossians 3:12 NASB)

In a world full of people who are hurting, who sin and are sinned against, who offend and are offended, we constantly see those who are distressed and dispirited. We see people all around us who carry the scars of the pains and burdens of this present age. To them, we are called to go in the grace of God and the power of the Holy Spirit – to be like Jesus!

To live out before others the compassion[35] we ourselves have received from Him. To show His compassion to those who like sheep have gone astray and point them to the Shepherd whose compassion is a healing balm for their hearts.

As His children, we must live so that the word that captures the heart of Christ might be displayed in us also.

## THE PEACE OF CHRIST

The peace of Christ is clearly thought of as that inward serenity which Christ bestows. In John 14:27, "Peace I leave with you, My peace I give to you." But this inward serenity is related to the cosmic "peace" (see 1:20) which God made through *the blood of His* Cross, in reconciling all things to Himself. It can therefore be regarded as the end for which Christians *were called in the one body*. There is a foreshadowing of the thought, which is developed in its fullness in Ephesians, that:

---

The divine unity of the Church of Christ is the pattern, or nucleus, about which the unity of the redeemed cosmos is *even now* taking shape!

---

The *divine unity* of the Church of Christ is the pattern, or rather the nucleus, about which the unity of the *redeemed* cosmos is even now taking shape! The universal harmony which God ordains to be the final state of His whole creation is to be reflected in the heart (love) of Christian believers everywhere!

Once again Paul calls for *thanksgiving* in the humble recognition that the love and peace of the Christian fellowship are not our achievement of which we might boast, but God's gracious gift to us in Christ. The same point is repeated twice again in the verses,

---

[35] *The Bible Knowledge Commentary says: The verb "to have compassion"* (splanchnizomai) *is used in the New Testament only by the Synoptic Gospel writers: five times in Matthew (9:36; 14:14; 15:32; 18:27; 20:34), four in Mark (1:41; 6:34; 8:2; 9:22), and three times Luke (7:13; 10:33; 15:20). Suggesting strong emotion, it means "to feel deep sympathy."*

suggesting that giving thanks to God is the culminating expression of the Christian's whole life before God (see 1:12).

The consistent determined purpose of Christian love takes all that a person has and the grace of God supporting that. The massive goodness of Christian character is seen not in the hard and self-assertive, but in those who have been mellowed, without being softened, by the love of God which Christ inspires. There is a severity in love that does not let us down but pulls us up. Notice the demands that the love of Christ lays upon us in the message which the apostle John addressed to the church at Laodicea, hard by Colossae, a generation after Paul wrote his Epistle to the Colossians (see Revelation 3:14-22). To this church, "neither cold nor hot," which had evidently lapsed into arrogant materialism, is addressed one of the tenderest invitations to loving fellowship with Christ to be found in all Scripture. "If any man hears my voice, and open the door, I will come into him, and will sup with him, and he with me." (see Revelation 3:20). But these words are immediately preceded by love's nonstop imperative, "As many as I love, I rebuke and chasten be zealous, therefore, and repent.

## THE INDWELLING WORD OF CHRIST

Let the word of Christ richly dwell within you ... (Colossians 3:16). The expression *Word of Christ* is not found elsewhere in the Pauline writings (in 1 Thessalonians 1:8, "the word of the Lord" undoubtedly means "the gospel." Paul in using this Greek term "logos of Christ" meaning "word." "The Word (Logos) was made flesh and dwelt among us." (see John 1:14)

As Christians we are confronted daily with a lot of strange talk about "thrones, or dominions, or principalities, or powers," "the elemental spirits of the universe," "worship of angels," "fullness of life," "Do not handle, Do not touch, Do not taste," used out of Christian context. If not careful much of this could be taught or pondered without any thought of Christ at all.

Paul urged the Colossians and us today, to get back to your center (Christ) in your religious instruction (**as you teach**); in your moral education (**admonish one another**); in your quest for culture and a well stored-up mind **(in all wisdom).** Abandon this contemporary fashion of thought. Some other philosophy "according to human tradition" will be in style tomorrow (study carefully Col. 2:8).

Get over the idea that you can find in the realm of *secular learning,* especially in the *pseudo learning* which has confused you, a more profound understanding of human destiny in the universe, and their duty in this world, than is offered in Christian biblical revelation. Fill your minds in the drama of our redemption as it is given in the gospel of Christ our Savior. (study prayerfully, 1 Corinthians 15:1-4).

God's first utterance in the work of creation was to give light. That was not because He needed it to do His work; no, the light was for us. Light enables us to see Him and to identify His fingerprints on the creation around us, to discern what is good from what is not, and to follow Jesus one step at a time in this vast world. Let the divine light of that revelation suffuse and illuminate the widest research of human thought with its unique moral and spiritual values.

It is reflected in the daily news as our institutions of higher learning are exposed by their (feelings oriented) thoughts projected as (a) truth, which is producing a type of leadership that is unfounded. We are seeing weakness in leadership at all levels of government, industry, science, and education because of the secular products our various schools of higher learning are sending forth to do this nation's business. They bend to a certain political persuasion – with the results of our kicking God and the things of God to the curb. He will have the last say!

Meanwhile, the cultivated postmodern mind will be not less scholarly, less educated, less intellectually free, **but more,** for heeding Paul's counsel, *Let the word of Christ dwell I you richly.*

# STUDY GUIDE: CHAPTER 15

1. We are called of the _____ of _____ and the power of the _____ _____ to be like Jesus.

2. The Peace of Christ (serenity) is related to the _____ peace.

3. God made through the _____ of His _____, in reconciling all things to Himself.

4. The divine unity of the church is the _____ or the _____ about which the unity of the _____ cosmos is even now taking place.

5. Giving thanks to God is the _____ expression of the Christian's whole life.

6. The determined purpose of Christian love cannot be fulfilled without the support of the _____ _____.

7. To what church did Christ direct the message "_____ are neither _____ nor _____."

# CHAPTER SIXTEEN

# Help Others To Follow Jesus

*"We proclaim Him, admonishing every person and teaching every person with all wisdom, so that we may present every person complete in Christ."* (Colossians 1:28 NASB)

Everything we need to know about doctrine is laid down in the Word of God. The Bible furnishes the minister of God with ammunition, power, and words for reproof. A good minister does not always preach doctrine – but also reproves and rebukes. The Gospel contains the message of correction – and a good minister of the Gospel preaches Bible doctrine, reproves from the Bible, and corrects error through the Gospel.

The preacher does not preach what he or she thinks, nor do they preach through catechisms or a book of doctrine; he or she preaches the Word of God-the Book, and laid down in holy Scripture is everything we need for instruction in righteousness. So God's preacher does not seek opinions concerning anything that has to do with right living and Bible doctrine; all the instruction we need is laid down in God's Holy Word.

It has been said, God's Word is a *tool chest* containing every tool we need for preaching – whether it be doctrine, reproof, correction, or instruction. The Word of God is a *complete food center:* In it we find all of the spiritual milk, meat, and bread that we need for spiritual growth. The Bible is a complete *clothing store:* It clothes us with salvation, the garments of sanctification, and the robe of righteousness. The Bible is a complete spiritual *Hospital:* It contains all necessary medications and instruments for strengthening and building up undernourished, sickly Christians.

The Bible contains anything, all things, and everything needed by God's minister to do a perfect job of preaching the Word in its entirety, winning sinners, feeding babes in Christ, strengthening the weak, and nourishing the strong and the full grown disciple. Everything God's minister needs is in the Bible.

One of the greatest needs in the pulpit today is for God's preachers to get back to the Bible and stop preaching man-made doctrine, man-made ideas, and man's programs. In these last and evil days, we need to get back to *"Thus saith the Lord"* in every phase of Gospel ministry.

No one has the right to interpret the Bible to fit his or her religious ideas.

Scriptures are not to be privately interpreted. The only way to understand the Word of God is to compare spiritual things with spiritual (see 1 Corinthians 2:11-13).

---

We will not adjust the Bible to the Age
but
We will adjust the Age to the Bible.

**PASTOR CHARLES SPURGEON**

---

# THE EXODUS CONTINUES

One of the major lessons we have learned in this season is the importance of getting the diagnosis right. We are hearing more frequently of people proceeding too quickly with medication before hearing back from the specialist. In many cases the treatment does more harm than good. I believe similarly, the local church has a discipleship disease (thinking that they have gotten too deep) so the church has become increasingly irrelevant and requires too much from people who want to get involved. So, we have develop strategies that:

- Require less of people
- Cut out essential Bible training ("teaching them to observe all things that I have commanded you").
- Focus on keeping disciples in the church – rather than growing disciples in the church.

- We have lowered the bar and we have settled for the lowest common denominator.
- We are asking too less of the people.
- We are giving people a shallow and generic spirituality.
- We view the pastor as a marketeer rather than a minister.

In order to treat this disease, we have accepted a remedy that does more harm than good. As a result:

Many of us have misdiagnosed the disease and are mistreating the church. The symptoms of our ministry disease are that:

- We are not too deep, but too shallow.
- People and students are leaving the church.
- Lack of maturing disciples.
- Decreased attendance.
- People are leaving because we are giving them too little.
- They are leaving because we have not given them any reason to stay.
- We are not too deep, but we are too trivial.
- We are treating the symptoms of the wrong disease.

People are leaving the church not because we are asking too much of them, but because we have not asked enough of them. They are leaving not because we have given them more Bible, but because we have given less Bible. We have taken the edge off what is meant to follow Christ. Simply put, we have settled for a shallow or no approach to discipleship, believing in *width* rather than *depth*. We have adopted philosophies of ministry that focus on *growing crowds* instead of *Christ followers of Jesus*.

We have asked our pastors to be *marketeers*, not *ministers of the Gospel*. In our churches we focus on keeping people – but if they want to grow, they have to go outside the church.

It is time for the church to ask some life-changing questions about our disease that we share with so many churches:

1. How can we create depth that might lead to breadth?
2. Can it be that the church should think about what it means to go deeper with fewer people or of going wider with the many?

3. What if our cultural concern is about what it means to the church to embody the depth and substance of the Christian faith – not a shallow spirituality that appeals to the masses?

4. What if we could think through a philosophy of ministry that helped people grow and mature into deep and holistic disciples?

5. What if we could develop and implement a philosophy of ministry that not only appeals to the lowest common denominator but created a *dissatisfaction with people staying there*?

6. What if we asked better questions about our philosophy of ministry that eventually led to the growth and flourishing of mature and holistic disciples in the context of the local church?

My hope and prayers are that local churches would grow in their faith in the Lord, that if we focus on growing disciples (as commanded to do) we will build the church – but if we focus on growing the church, we may neglect growing disciples. As holistic disciples are being shaped and formed in the context of the local church, we need to be intentional about sending (all of the church) into their spheres of influence to make more disciples. Discipleship never stops with a disciple; all disciples are called to go make more disciples. (see 2 Timothy 2:2)

That's where any conversation about discipling others must begin – in remembering what it means to follow Jesus. Discipling means *helping others* to follow Jesus. Discipling is a *relationship* in which we seek to do spiritual enhancement for someone by initiating, teaching, correcting, modeling, loving, humbling ourselves, counseling, and influencing. How then do we disciple? First of all, the Bible tasks all of us with this work:

- John tells us to love one another (see 2 John 5).
- Paul tells us to encourage and build-up one another (see 1 Thessalonians 5:11)
- He also tells us to encourage one another and build up one another, since we want to see everyone mature in Christ (see Colossians 1:28).

- Hebrews tells us to consider to stir up one another to love and good works (see Hebrews 10:24). You must choose who you are going to engage.

In his book *Discipling – How to help others follow Jesus*, Mark Dever give nine factors to consider in deciding those to whom you will go:

1. Family member
2. Spiritual state
3. Church membership
4. Gender
5. Age
6. Different from you
7. Teachability
8. Faithfulness to teach others (2 Timothy 2:2)
9. Proximity[36]

Your success in ministering is found in building disciples – who love God with all of their heart, soul, strength, and mind (see Luke 10:27). Christ is the goal, not better or more impressive ministries. **He is what we want!**

---

[36] Mark Dever *Discipling – How to Help Others Follow Christ*, (Crossway Publishers 2016) 78

# STUDY GUIDE: CHAPTER 16

1. Everything we need to know about _____
   is laid down in the _____ of _____.
2. The Gospel contains the _____.
3. The Bible contains everything needed for feeding babes in
   Christ, strengthening _____ _____, and
   moving the _____ and _____ _____.
4. No one has the right to _____ the Bible to fit his or
   her _____ _____.
5. God's preachers do not seek _____ concerning
   _____ that has to do with _____
   _____ and _____.
6. Discipling means _____ _____ to
   _____ _____.
7. We need to get back to "_____ _____
   _____ in every phase of Gospel ministry.

# A FINAL WORD

Reaching cultural Christians with the true gospel requires holy boldness. The boldness needed to reach them is one that doesn't fear social consequences. Perhaps you have cultural Christian friends or relatives who claim to be Christians, but know there is something different about you. To ask them what that difference is, it's just that you are a little more "into" church and religion. However, you have to let them know that what they are seeing is someone who loves and believes the gospel of Jesus Christ. Our own personal striving for Christ and the enjoyment of His great grace are powerful witnessing tools. In everything we must point to Jesus Christ. Paul tells us in 1 Corinthians 13:1,

> *"If I speak in the tongues of men and of angels, but have not love, I am a noisy gong or a clanging cymbal."* (ESV)

We have to reach out to cultural Christians in our *spheres of influence*, honestly and lovingly telling our friends, loved ones, and fellow employees who claim Christianity that they might be missing Christ and the true gospel. Certainly, this will no doubt offend a cultural Christian, but if the relationship is there – tell them the truth.

## LOVE GOD AND LOVE HIS CHURCH

Jesus made clear that we show love for Him by obeying His commands (see John 14:15). But we also see descriptions throughout Scripture of adoring God, praising Him, glowing in His grace. A *maturing heart in Christ* will grow more and more loving as it beholds our loving God. Additionally, we seek to love what God loves, His glory and His church:

- Continuously, we see calls to urgency in pushing one another on to good works (see Hebrews 10:24).
- Continue to speak only what benefits others (see Ephesians 4:29).

- Consider 7 others more important than ourselves (Philippians 2:3).
- Continue to do good to all people, especially our Christian brothers and sisters (see Galatians 6:10).

The Psalms are full of adoring praises to God and the New Testament epistles are full of guidelines for interpersonal relations within the body of believers. Both promote love and consideration above selfishness. Amen!

Printed in the United States
by Baker & Taylor Publisher Services